15 Ways to Own Your Future

Take Control of Your Destiny in Business & in Life

T0158657

15 Ways to Own Your Future

Take Control of Your Destiny in Business & in Life

Michael Khouri

BUSINESS
BOOKS

Winchester, UK
Washington, USA

First published by Business Books, 2016
Business Books is an imprint of John Hunt Publishing Ltd., Laurel House, Station Approach,
Alresford, Hants, SO24 9JH, UK
office1@jhpbooks.net
www.johnhuntpublishing.com

For distributor details and how to order please visit the 'Ordering' section on our website.

Text copyright: Michael Khouri 2015

ISBN: 978 1 78535 300 0
Library of Congress Control Number: 2015954376

A CIP catalogue record for this book is available from the British Library.

Design: Stuart Davies

Printed and bound by CPI Group (UK) Ltd, Croydon, CR0 4YY, UK

We operate a distinctive and ethical publishing philosophy in all
areas of our business, from our global network of authors to
production and worldwide distribution.

CONTENTS

Preface

You only have so much energy;
expend it where it will have the most impact

This long version, how-to book gave birth to my first published book, *The Power of Ownership,* which accentuated *15 Ways to Own Your Future* in short-story form.

As a short story, *The Power of Ownership* conveyed the message that we make choices every day that define our life. Life will provide its pain. We decide, alone, based on our perspective, whether it translates to suffering. We also decide and determine our enjoyment and triumphs long before we experience them, through our perspective.

The start of this book may very well have been initiated almost fifty years ago, during a period in my life when I was faced with a major challenge. I was a typical sixteen-year-old. I was trying to make the transition from boy to man. Sixteen is an age when everything seems more dramatic than it really is. Having my own car, impressing the girls, and excelling in sports, was all that mattered. My ability to be very effective at all of them, at the same time, was more important than it should have been. Whether it was these important issues or something else that caused my problem, is not relevant. What is relevant was the repercussion of placing so much significance on my success and an inability to put it all in perspective. It was eating me alive.

Unfortunately, what had become nothing more than emotion had begun to produce some nasty physical effects. I developed a disease called ulcerative colitis, which for the most part was an unknown disease at the time. One of the factors that impacted this disease was believed to be stress. My stress, which was self-induced, centered on an inability to put things in perspective.

This disease caused so much damage to my system that by the

1

time I turned seventeen, I had no choice but to finally go to the hospital for a diagnosis. I had lost so much blood that my body was not too far from closing down.

I was told there was no cure for this disease. I was also told that it would never leave my body and that any major responsibilities, because of the stress, could kill me. I was told that the only way to limit the impact was to talk through any issues bothering me. Neither solution thrilled me. My doctor also gave me a major dose of horse-size pills.

After about three years of taking sixteen of these horse pills a day, going to the doctor for monthly check-ups, and being quizzed about my stress level, I had reached my limit. I woke up one morning around my twentieth birthday and decided I was done with this routine.

Fortunately, my solution was positive driven. I simply decided that I was going to heal myself. It was my belief no doctor and no number of pills could do this for me. In order for it to happen, I had to do it myself. Beyond that, I was tired of going to the doctor every month. I had taken enough medication to last me a lifetime. I called the hospital and cancelled my appointment for that week. I told them they would not be seeing me anymore. I also refused to refill my prescription. I saw pill prescriptions as nothing more than an unfulfilling panacea.

I had come to the conclusion, at the early age of twenty, that most things in life are defined by perspective. As a result, I could believe whatever I wanted to. I would choose to take an optimistic outlook on everything going forward. My first optimistic assessment was to declare that I was cured. I no longer needed to see the doctor for this disease, because it no longer existed! As many people before me have stated: "The mind is a powerful tool." I declared myself empowered. I had the authority. I was now in control.

I did not realize it at the time, but I had experienced a life-altering moment the day I decided I had had enough and took control. I decided I was going to enjoy every moment and direct my own destiny. I would no longer be adversely affected by any difficult event thrown at me. I was going to enjoy life to its fullest, and with this newfound perspective, look for the positive in everything.

I have taken no medications for the last forty-three years and have only been to the hospital for a check-up twice. During that period of time, I have taken on major responsibilities as a husband, father of two daughters, and served in many executive positions managing hundreds of people in high-profile industries.

I feel very fortunate for having found this long-term perspective early in life. Many people never recognize the moment because they are too engulfed in where they aren't. This makes it very difficult to enjoy the moment for what it is. Memories become defined as something only in the past as opposed to what is happening today.

This definition of most people's self-imposed anxiety is something that too many just accept as "being life." It is as though we spend our lives just standing on a railroad track staring ahead. We expect that train to hit us head-on and fulfill that self-induced prophecy. If we get frozen in anticipation of bad things happening, they usually do.

This collision image of life may be exaggerated to a certain extent, but the overall feeling of lack of control that it conveys is more common in most people's perception of life than it should be. Life does not have to be viewed as a constant calamity that self-perpetuates, nor does it have to be actually lived in that way.

This brings to mind a disturbing conversation I overheard recently in a restaurant while in a meeting with a former employee. It was not the close proximity that allowed me to overhear this conversation. They were talking very loud. One man, who appeared to be in his mid-forties, was telling his friend that he hated his job, and that nothing ever went right. This revelation appeared to surprise the other man, who I assumed was a friend. After listening for a while, it became clear that he could not have been a long-time friend, because he appeared surprised by the admission. His response gave the impression that he was not prepared for such a personal confession.

"Oh really," he stated, with some discomfort in his voice.

This man who hated his job went on to say that he, in fact, hated to get out of bed. He added, "I'd rather be sleeping because that is the only time I feel okay."

The man who now was trying to help the depressed man replied, "What is causing all of this stress? Is it primarily the job?"

"Yes and no," he lamented. He confessed that nothing was going well at home or at work.

The empathizing man asked the depressed man what he would do if he were fired today, and if he had recently looked for another job. The depressed man answered very quickly that it was too hard to find a job, and if he were fired he did not know what he would do. This conversation continued for around thirty minutes. The surprised man was not sure where to go with the conversation. The depressed man continued to talk about the hopelessness he was feeling. Even though I had arrived before them, I also left before them. The conversation repeated itself with no apparent end in sight, while I put the gratuity on the table and walked away.

What was very clear was that this depressed individual had a feeling of total despair. He was nowhere near having any control over what was happening in his life. His chances of changing this in the near future appeared slim. But there was one thing he was very certain about. His world was a living "hell" and he saw no way out. What kind of certainty is this to live with?

It has often been stated that the only certainties in life are death and taxes. They are the two things we are very comfortable predicting with some conviction. The implication in this message is not pretty by any stretch of the imagination. Inherent in this negative perspective is a total feeling of lack of control. It may not be to the extent of the depressed man in the restaurant, but it is way up there on the submission scale.

Control, or lack thereof, has inspired many debates on "pre-ordained versus hard work and earned results." Many are comfortable with destiny since it takes a heavy burden off one and transfers it elsewhere. If everything is predetermined at birth and we have no control over anything, the only responsibility we have in life is to go through the motions and take what is given.

Taking responsibility for one's path carries the burden of ownership, and as such it is not so endearing to most. Acknowledgment implies that the results we achieve, or don't achieve, in life, primarily happiness, are a product of our own doing.

It is not only in work or in business where a rejection of accountability has taken a major foothold. It has unfortunately been applied to anything associated with the core person, where everything has its basis. When a person hands off responsibility for anything that happens to him in life, he also passes on full responsibility for his own self-esteem. The resulting self-esteem is most often not very high. This statement has a tendency to invite the debate about the pros and cons of religion. That debate is a non-factor relative to this philosophy. One does not discount the other. It does not mean that religion has no place in one's life. Religion is based on faith and does not surrender all responsibility to a higher being. Religion acknowledges that in order to receive our final reward, we must take responsibility for our actions. Within that faith is an acknowledgement that we have some control.

It is also understood that there are things that happen in life that appear out of our control. That fact does not conflict with full responsibility. We cannot control death nor can we eliminate taxes, but we can control how we deal with death and taxes.

Most often, it is not the circumstances in life that cause one problems, it is how one deals with circumstances.

In almost forty years in business, I have seen people accomplish many things through a willingness to take ownership. Was it their destiny also?

I believe that there can be a co-existence between destiny and ownership. But that co-existence works only if destiny is used as a motivational tool as opposed to being based on an it-is-or-it-isn't factor. In more defined terms, an individual sees a certain vision, makes decisions that impact fulfillment, and works through the obstacles in life in order to achieve the vision.

Also, there is a direct correlation between results and happenstance, as implied in the statement "things happen for a reason." When we learn from a bad experience, we put ourselves in a position of being prepared for opportunities. By learning and preparing, we align ourselves in a position to take advantage of those opportunities. It is only with determination, ownership, and good results achieved, that we can look back at those bad things as having happened for a reason. Nothing, for the most part, is just given to us. We have to earn what we gain. We earn what we gain by taking charge.

There is another way to look at this "destiny versus taking charge" debate and make some logical sense out of it. When it comes down to basic participation in life, we actually have choices. We can either refuse to accept ownership for what happens to us, or we can take ownership. We either acknowledge we have no control or we take control.

This book, *15 Ways to Own Your Future*, is a recipe for controlling your own destiny. It suggests 15 Ways to Take Control of Your Destiny in Business and Life. If there is one point that becomes clear, it is the perspective that connects them. Each one affects the other fourteen.

If you utilize one of the Ways, the others become natural

extensions. It is an overall perspective that everyone can put into practice if they want to.

These 15 Ways are key beliefs I have learned, used, and shared with others over the last forty years. These concepts are not new, but as an interacting group they are new. Their impact on perspective and results can be significant. It is a summary based on my experiences and opinion on the best way to take control of your life and to enjoy life. I pass these on as a group because they are interacting approaches. They are what I have witnessed as an individual, business executive, spouse, and father. I offer them as tried and true suggestions.

I also believe that the constant personal and business challenges demand that we find some feeling of control in order to get the most out of life. Embracing these 15 Ways will not assure success, nor eliminate failure. There is no sure way to eliminate failure in some form, but that is not a bad thing. I have had many successes in life, and I have had my share of failures. I have learned as much, if not more, from my failures.

The bottom-line objective should be to grow and prosper both emotionally and intellectually. Most importantly, we want to enjoy the ride along the way. We cannot eliminate the pressures that come in life, business or personal. However, we can learn how to put these pressures in perspective and reduce the resulting stress. We can learn how to get the most out of those personal and business relationships in our lives.

Pressure is really a state of mind. At times it can be more perception-based than reality-based. However, perceiving equals believing, and what we believe is what is real to us. When our perception has at its core a victim mentality, we only magnify this pressure. It is important that we control this process as opposed to letting it control us.

With the pressures you face today, with so much to balance and with employment security being a thing of the past, you must believe you have some control. The only way to believe you have control is to take control. This book is about taking control.

Finally, I must add that this book is based wholly on opinion and a value system I believe is critical to enjoyment. These values and approaches are combined with some supported "substantiated facts." However, these messages are driven more by trusted and applied beliefs. The problem with social "substantiated facts" is that most are subjective, and as such they are limited by the extent they are accepted. This self-interpretation is also deeply rooted in preconceived perceptions. The result is that facts are only facts if they are recognized as such by the receiver.

This book makes no claims of documented "facts." It adds only a great deal of theory, which really is the only information available relative to the topics discussed in this book. It again is also simply a promulgation of suggestions and opinions founded on one person's enjoyment of life, nothing more and nothing less. I do believe these suggestions will lead to better collaboration, create better work/life integration and flexibility, and help one become a self-mentor.

Summary

Recognize the things you cannot control.

Impact those things you can control.

Learn how to work through those things you cannot control.

Chapter 1

The Work/Home Environment

Things do not happen for a reason; it only seems that way
after we have made our own opportunity

Over the last thirty years we have seen dramatic changes take
place in the world, from the definition of the family, to the definition of the workplace. We have seen major technological
changes that have impacted the way we communicate in
business and in our personal lives. While all this has been
happening, we have seen the population of the United States
increase to over 300 million people. We have also seen our
population become much more diverse, with immigration
adding millions to our number and diversity to our social and
work environments.

With the technological advances in wireless, computers, and
robotics we have seen an increasing dependence on "screen"
communication displacing "eyeball-to-eyeball/one-on-one"
direct communication. We now communicate more by screen.
Ironically, our desire to connect intimately with others in order
to elevate self-esteem has been magnified significantly. We have
become accustomed to communicating from a distance while
craving the need to be individually recognized and appreciated.

The end result of all of these changes (which certainly would
take more than a book to define) has brought businesses and
individuals to a point where there is more to do than we have the
time to accomplish.

The impact over the last twenty years from the emergence of
women in more business leadership roles has been huge. As a
result, we have a wider, more rounded, thought-provoking,
creative, and exhilarating perspective in the work environment

today.

The "good old boy" environment has been challenged, and even though not entirely replaced, is not the foundation of all business cultures today.

With each new generation entering the workforce, there is a new psyche that continues to evolve. We are beginning to see the work/home demands increase as the need for more quantity and improved quality scribbles the line between gender responsibilities and work/home responsibilities. With 24/7 communication capability enhancement, the line between work and home continues to get grayer. We are now advancing to more of a work/life integration acknowledgment which looks at the achievement of balance at another level.

We have evolved with a more diverse population as a whole into a world made smaller by a global economy. Enhanced communication technology and improved travel has resulted in worldwide mergers and acquisitions. For many, trying to slow down uncontrollable increased responsibilities and distractions has become an all-consuming challenge.

With this perpetual change there is one thing that continues to stay the same. It is the desire of people to feel a sense of control while maintaining and sustaining some measure of self-esteem. Alphonse Karr said in 1849, "The more things change, the more they remain the same." This may apply more today than it did in 1849.

We have begun to see a thirst for finding a way to get the most out of everything we do while finding a way to enjoy what we do at the same time. As much as things have changed over the last thirty years, both socially and in the business environment, basic individual needs have not changed. Purpose, enjoyment of others, and responsibilities with redeeming value are still high priorities.

We are constantly told that the value system has been overturned and that ruthlessness and deceit have replaced respect, integrity, and a good work ethic. Nothing could be further from the truth.

We are continually fed through headlines in print, the Internet, and on television news that doing the right thing the right way no longer applies. It is not true.

We are led to believe that the world is overrun with cynics, and that cynicism and skepticism are the new creed. We are led to believe that doubt should be the first reaction when interacting with another individual or when receiving any form of communication.

All of the above-mentioned phenomena may certainly have some basis, but this feeling of despair and acceptance will certainly not advance an individual's success in any facet of his or her life. Nor will it help you achieve any sense of enjoyment.

The messages in this book are not only important individually. Practicing them as a whole will help produce long-lasting relationships, purpose, and success in every facet of your life.

There is a way to approach work, home, your health, and to appreciate yourself along with others. There is a way to get through the obstacles and challenges and circumstances that you face on a daily basis and come out on top. There is a way to continually move forward and attain a higher level of satisfaction. There is a way to build a network that opens more opportunities than you could ever imagine. There is a way to get in control and get the most out of life.

The next fifteen chapters are a brief and viable summary of the approaches and values you can use to achieve more enjoyment in everything you do. They will help you gain a sense of control in a world that on the surface seems to be twirling out of control. The *15 Ways* discussed in these chapters will also help you better achieve collaboration in the work environment, along with aiding in the creation of a better micro-work environment.

Chapter 2

A Positive Perspective

A positive perspective does not insure success;
it improves learning, which is a prerequisite to success

Have you ever been around people who see the negative in everything? The first thing you will notice, beyond them being a great prophesier when it comes to their own destiny, is that most people do not enjoy being near them. It is no coincidence that their "sky is falling" mentality always turns out to be true for them. The reason for the sky always falling is that they self-consciously do everything they can to make sure things fall apart—and as such, they do.

If these negative-thinking individuals put as much thought and effort into focusing on positive achievement, they might be amazed at the good results they achieved. **The first Way to Take Control of Your Destiny in Business and Life is to have a positive perspective.**

This key Way can lead to better collaboration because most people enjoy working closely with people who bring a positive perspective to any project or discussion.

As a general manager in a growing industry for many years, I had a market manager who reported to me who used negativity to the limit in his perspective. When I would make my weekly call to him or visit him for a few days, his negative view on how things were going or the direction they were going was more than I could take.

This negative perspective on the present and the future existed while managing in an industry that was still in the maturation process. Most markets were experiencing 20% to 40% annual revenue increases. He was a carryover from a previous company owner and his "Who Moved My Cheese" attitude was not moving forward.

I can clearly say that in my over thirty-five years of managing people through change associated with acquisitions, mergers, and restructuring, a positive perspective is what separated those who made a smooth adjustment from those who could not accept the change.

I have always been described as a very positive person, but even I was having difficulty moving this manager's perspective forward. When I asked for any analysis or assessment of how things were going, I could count on him to give me the worst scenario possible. He could give me a million reasons why business was not good, and most of them had to do with changes he could not adjust to. His staff was not optimistic about the state of business either. What a surprise!

What was even more tragic about his poor perspective was that he was a nice person. I enjoyed spending time with him when I could look past his business perspective. Unfortunately, I was not there to make friends. My job was to maximize the results from the business in every market, period.

After a year of banging my head against the wall, trying to get this guy to be more positive and using all of the positive strategy I had in my arsenal, I actually had made some progress.

I walked in one day for what I thought was a surprise visit. As it turned out, I was the one who received the surprise. He had made the decision that adapting to the new company was not going to happen, and that it was best he move on to something else. He had come up with a solution as opposed to finding more reasons things couldn't be done. This was the most positive change I had seen from him from the day he first reported to me. He was resigning. It was not a coincidence that I had finally seen enough of his "no solution" approach to everything. I was on the verge of letting him go, and really should have pulled the trigger before he did.

He had wasted a year focusing on why things were so bad and how nothing he could do would change the results. His reports on how bad things were and why there were no solutions took tremendous effort and energy. He could not see how this approach to running the business in his market was affecting his poor results. As far as he could tell, it wasn't his fault he wasn't having any success. He had reasoned there was no point in trying to find solutions when none existed.

The truth was that he neither had the motivation nor did he want to get the motivation necessary for improving things. Even more significant was the issue that finding solutions would require him to be part of the solution. It must have been easier to just be part of the problem. Also, by telling himself there were no solutions, he did not have to worry about failure.

He was a classic example of how it takes less effort to watch things fall apart than it does to put in the effort to make things succeed. Just as significant, it also shows how it is less painful to accept failure when no effort is given. Stated another way, it is one thing to expect failure and get it, but quite another thing to expect success and get failure.

There is a long history of many men and women who after failure have gone on to achieve significant success. Most of these acknowledged achievers continued to battle and would not abandon their goals no matter how bleak things looked.

It is important to realize that it takes not only failure, but also learning from failure, to achieve success. Positive-thinking people learn how to put their failures in perspective and they learn from their failures. They recognize that failure will get them closer to success with the next effort. Looking for bad outcomes is not what positive thinkers anticipate. They just learn to deal with it when it happens. They realize failure will happen along the way.

There are many stories about events that have gone bad (which are easy to find) that unfortunately enforce this belief that in the end, all things will go bad. Our news networks feed off this mentality. You might say that Murphy is not only well-known but also honored by his saying "Whatever can go wrong, will go wrong."

Have you ever taken the time to track the news you hear, read, or see over a week's time from the Internet, radio, television, or newspaper? It is frightening! Here are the headlines taken from one news web page on a given day. I don't need to mention which web page because any website, newspaper, or television news on this particular day would be dominated by the same stories:

Brownie: I screwed up, Chertoff screwed up worse
Record sentence sought for crooked congressman
Hamas takes hard line on international stage
Former pop star jailed for child abuse
Bathroom break ban teaches teacher a lesson
Cell phone bandit: "My whole life is ruined"
Fugitive dad with sick son's kidney might be in Mexico
Mine survivor will "roll his eyes" at attention
"20th hijacker" claims torture made him lie

These were nine out of twelve headlines. The only two that could be considered in the realm of positive information were not actually news items. These nine don't exactly bring a ray of sunshine into your day. It is hard to feel good after being subjected to this kind of news. Think about the fact that we are subjected to this kind of news daily, 24 hours a day, and 365 days a year. If you were to take a random thirty-minute analysis of your local news any day in any week, you would find more of the same. Your local news would update you on local murders, burglaries, car accidents, and crimes of every kind, mixed in with disheartening national stories. We literally get a perpetual feeding of bad news that has no end. Is it any wonder that seeing people smiling is not very common? Optimism takes a perpetual beating daily in our lives.

The need for an optimistic outlook as a cushion to all of the perpetual negative news should not be underestimated. Maintaining optimism is the only road to progress.

I recently walked through an entertainment and service business just to get a gauge on the environment before meeting with the general manager. Since this was an entertainment establishment, it could be assumed that the employees' focus would be on enhancing the customer experience. Is that a fair expectation of an entertainment facility? I would certainly think so.

During this thirty-minute walk-through, I came in close contact with nearly thirty employees. These employees, who were taking care of a customer's needs or just walking by me, had one clear thing in common: they did not smile and their persona left the impression they did not want to be there. I don't know what was more shocking, that I did not see one person smile or that this was an entertainment facility!

These people obviously did not enjoy their jobs. However, I have the feeling that they did not smile regularly outside of the facility either. Is it the news and events in our daily life that causes this sadness or is it more related to an inability to put things in perspective?

How much responsibility do we have for our own morale?

In spite of the fact that the news we watch, listen to, or see on the Internet is dominated by negativity, we, individually, control the volume. We also determine to what extent we wish to be impacted. Certainly, one could argue that bad news is more interesting and, as such, gets more attention. That does not mean that we all don't want to feel better at the end of the day.

I'm sure most psychologists would say that watching bad news makes us feel a little better about our own situations. That is why we are interested in hearing about other people's misfortunes. However, it is one thing to watch, listen, or read in an unattached way and feel better about one's own situation. It is another to confront the negativity "eyeball to eyeball" that seeps into one's own space.

The first way to take control of your life is to have a positive perspective about your environment, while at the same time believing that things can always get better. This is not only the key to always improving your own situation. It has been proven that it goes a long way in helping one maintain good health. It is a characteristic I have always looked for when hiring people and I still do.

Like anything else, there is no way to achieve perfection. Not everybody who worked for me maintained a constant positive perspective. But, those who did were more successful in their careers and from what I could see also had happier home lives.

In an article written by Del Jones in a 2005 issue of *USA Today* titled "Optimism Puts Rose-Colored Tint in Glasses of Top Execs," he stated that "the quality most common to those at the top is their tendency to see everything through rose-colored glasses." He added, "Leaders, it seems, are more optimistic than the rest of us curmudgeons."

The article went on to say:

Survey after survey indicates this. When 50,000 workers were asked, 54% of senior managers said they viewed their organizations as "healthy," according to a Booz Allen Hamilton survey released last month. But just 33% of middle managers and less than 30% of the rank and file echoed the sentiment.

Senior managers are overly optimistic, even about their own careers. When executive job search firm ExecuNet this year asked 1,500 executives how long they expected to be at their present job the average answer was 5.4 years. In reality their tenure has slipped to 3.6 years on average from 4.1 years in 2002. Last month there were 118 CEO departures vs. 46 in November 2004, according to outplacement firm Challenger

Gray & Christmas.

The glass-half-full thinking spills over into just about everything. Sirota Survey Intelligence, which specializes in measuring employee attitudes, crunched data from 293,000 employees for *USA Today* and found that senior managers were more optimistic about almost everything at work, from teamwork to the speed of their own performance. A National Urban League survey of 5,500 workers last year found that 47% of executives think their companies had an effective diversity program vs. 32% of all employees.

The article goes on to add that according to Marcus Buckingham, author of *The One Thing You Need to Know*, "The opposite of a leader isn't a follower. The opposite of a leader is a pessimist."

In an article written by Robyn Greenspan in April 2013, she reports:

> Corporate business leaders are emphasizing the importance of cultural fit and think a positive attitude can have a great effect on team morale, particularly as economic factors cause companies to struggle with employee engagement and motivation. Nearly 88 of the senior-level executives recently surveyed by ExecuNet said they would rather enhance their team with that individual who possesses a good attitude, even if he or she does not perform to the highest level or have top qualifications. Only six percent of the surveyed executives said they would accept an A-player's bad attitude, and another six percent were unsure.

Based on these surveys of executives, it clearly seems possible that the way to move up the corporate ladder is to be a positive person. One could conclude that it is this positive makeup that allows an executive to find a positive outlook in the dynamics of any situation.

It can also be stated there is always some positive that can be found in any situation. Finding a positive doesn't mean reality is ignored. It is a matter of believing in solutions as opposed to accentuating obstacles.

This again goes back to the old debate on a cup being half empty or half full. It is all a matter of perspective. In all day-to-day occurrences, where there is some bad, there is always some good, if we take the time to look. Sometimes the good is not immediately apparent. It may even take time for the good to come to the surface.

The key in any situation is to look for the positive, and with that perspective you will find it. This can be as simple as learning something new. Learning something new may not prevent a recurrence, but at the very least wisdom can be gained. On that very limited basis, there has been some good that has resulted.

With a positive outlook and a clear direction, handling setbacks or meeting challenges takes on new meaning. It becomes a means to an end. When present setbacks or events are seen as just steps to a long-term vision, they no longer become life-defining moments.

Take a step back and look at all of the important things and important people in your life. Think about all of the positive things you can say about each situation and each person, and focus on those. Every person is blessed with both good attributes and questionable attributes. No situation is always all positive or all negative. The key is to focus on the good, while realistically looking at what you can do to make things better. There are some things that you just cannot impact. It is important to recognize what these are so you can save your energy for things you can impact. Not recognizing limitations just adds to a feeling of frustration and irritation.

The focus needs to be on the good and those things where you can have a positive influence. By taking this approach to every situation and every significant person in your life, you will feel better about yourself and ultimately your life as a whole. Think positive. Be an optimist. Look for the good in things as opposed to always the bad. You will find that this positive perspective will make you feel much better.

It has been stated by many successful people that success is contagious. The same can be said for optimism.

Setbacks and rough situations happen to everybody. It is not the circumstances that cause you problems. It is how you deal with the circumstances! These setbacks have to be looked at as nothing more than stages in a step-by-step approach to your ultimate goal. They become something that must happen in order to fulfill your vision.

If there is one thing we all have in common, it is having expectations fall short one time or another in our lives. It might be unfulfilled expectations in our careers or unfulfilled and unrealistic expectations we have of others. We have all had projects that did not bring the closure we anticipated and had something we wanted not happen.

We have all had to interact at some point with an individual who we did not like or who we felt was out to undermine us. These situations can impact the way we see things in the present and in the future. They can impact our perspective on the past, which can carry over to the present and future if we let it.

The healthiest conclusion we can arrive at in our assessment of all these common events is to try to look at them as learning experiences, not just experiences. If we recognize that anything that happens to us can be a stepping stone to something greater, something greater happens. If we look at every individual we interact with as a learning opportunity, we are more able to enjoy that interaction. We will be wiser.

Always believe that you will work things out for the best. Believe there is nothing you can't do. It will make you do everything you can to make it happen.

Don't worry about failure; it is just a step along the way to achieving a major accomplishment. We only have so many years to live on this earth, and the time that we have goes quickly. We have nothing to lose and everything to gain by staying optimistic along the way. Having a positive perspective, at the very least, will help you enjoy the time you have. The best it can do is help you accomplish any goal you ever wanted in life. Optimism against all odds is what separates those who enjoy life to its fullest from those who go through life in pain.

The Positive Pyramid

Results   *Success*

Plan/Execution   *Action*

Belief—"You Can Do It"   *Perspective*

Belief: The perspective that you can do whatever you focus on. You are in control.

Action: Look for the positive in situations. Execution is:

The vehicle we use to drive our beliefs

Acting with confidence

Anticipating success

Results: When beliefs and actions come together to produce success.

Success re-enforces beliefs which continue to make us act accordingly.

The cycle perpetuates itself.

Summary

Anticipate that something will be learned from every situation.

Look at difficult situations as a necessary means to a positive end.

Approach everything with a "can do" perspective. Positive thinking can impact your health.

Chapter 3

Have Balance in Your Life

"Wherever you are, be there"

Having balance in your life does not mean having good equilibrium. Although, with the overload we have coming at us in today's world, being able to stand up straight is not a bad start. Having balance means focusing on more than just one thing at a time while giving all you should to each need. Try to give proportionately to all of those things and people that are important in your life. That includes family, work, friends, health, and yourself. The priority can change at times based on unforeseen events and needs. **Balance is the second Way to Take Control of Your Destiny in Business and Life.**

A good way to make sure that you give proper focus on a consistent basis to all areas of your life is to set daily goals for each area. At the same time, it is important to recognize that technology has made this very difficult. Balance for most is best achieved through work/life integration. With more flexible work arrangements this balance becomes more viable. Work and personal become more defined by immediate priority as opposed to specific time, and more interchangeable as a result.

Most of us have heard sometime in our business career from a supervisor that creating a priority to-do list is the only way to get things done. This should also apply to things you want to accomplish at home and personally.

When you write goals down for all areas of your life, it serves as a reminder to spread your focus, while monitoring your ability to do so. Your goals for the day at work might be to finish a certain project and make certain calls, or resolve a transaction that needs closure. Home goals for a day might be to fix a leaky faucet, reconcile your bank statement, or make sure you spend quality time with your child. A personal goal may be to exercise for thirty minutes, finish a few chapters of a book, or get eight hours of sleep. Listing goals in writing will better insure that they get accomplished, and that they cover a wider distribution of areas in your life.

In terms of accomplishing long-term goals for the year or over a longer period, you have a much better chance of achievement if you write them down. You can take this a step further by making others aware of your goals. Making other people aware of your goals not only can make them seem more real, it insures that you will be asked at some point about your progress. You are holding yourself accountable. Making others aware of your goals increases the commitment to achievement. You are no longer just answering to yourself in terms of your success. If your commitment falters, you are not the only one who will be aware.

A good place to start in this process is to get an understanding of your current time distribution. You must understand how your time is being distributed between work, home, and self before you can outline a strategic plan and set goals accordingly.

A helpful exercise I use in one of my presentations with groups is to have people place a percentage of time they believe they spend on work, home, and themselves. Sleep and exercise fall under the category of self because it is something we do for ourselves. I have the participants calculate these percentages based on a normal 168-hour week.

I then ask five volunteers to give me their percentages. I then put the percentages on a board and figure an average for the five people. Not surprisingly, home and self usually take a pretty good beating while work is stated as having the highest percentage. In a healthy balanced life, I believe that all three categories should be fairly even, in the low to mid-thirties.

It is amazing how perception can influence perspective when someone is assessing his or her life. Perception becomes a person's reality. As an example, in a recent group seminar, one person actually believed that 80% of her week was spent on work. This made the other percentages inconsequential. After I asked a few questions, she quickly realized the percentages she gave were based more on feeling than fact. To her, it felt like her whole life centered on work.

If a person gets at least seven hours of sleep each night, exercises only a few hours a week, and does some reading or watching television, it can easily add up to around 56 hours. Take a 45-hour work week and factor in some work also done outside the office, and it can quickly add up to around 56 hours. The remainder should include time spent with family or friends—dining, going to school events, or participating in some other form of entertainment. These home hours should add up to around 56 hours. The hours in each category can tip one way or another from time to time, but over a period of time they should balance out pretty close to 33% for each category.

There is some reality to factor in. For some people, this calculation may look nothing close to an even distribution. This could explain a feeling that something seems missing in one's life. What one may realize quickly is that when the scale tilts to an extreme in any way, something is being affected in his or her life. If the scale tilts completely to the work category, they might be experiencing symptoms of burnout. They might have limited interaction with friends or family and/or unhealthy eating habits, and little time for exercise. This can even occur when one has more of an accepted work/life integration that acknowledges the ability to focus on a priority basis. The scale can still tip more to one side than another, if not out of control.

We have all had periods in our lives when we experienced some degree of burnout. I have been there, and I not only remember it well, I remember trying to formulate a plan to eliminate it. Symptoms I can recall are chronic fatigue, shortness of breath, and an inability to get a full night's sleep.

During that work-related burnout, I was fully aware I needed to make some changes. There was no way I was going to let my positive perspective, nor my achievement of balance and enjoyment of life, be affected. It is during these times that the importance of balance really comes to the forefront. It is during these times that the work/life integration process is not working as it should. A better balance in work/life integration suddenly becomes an immediate goal.

One area that has a tendency to get short-changed during these burnout periods is sleep. Stress and lack of sleep linked together can produce a perpetual vicious cycle. Stress leads to sleepless nights and sleepless nights lead to more unproductive days. It becomes difficult to determine which one is the product and which one is the by-product. According to a recent publication by the National Sleep Foundation:

Poor sleep and sleepiness cause disruptions in nearly every facet of one's life.

Sleep-related issues are cited as the most common reason people are late for work. Almost 3 in 10 working adults say they have missed work, events/activities or made errors at work because of sleep-related issues in the past three months.

Over an approximate six-month period while meeting with owners, CEOs, and general managers, I was shocked at the stress the majority of these people showed. I was willing to bet most of the stress was work related. That overwhelmed feeling I detected in them showed in their presentation and in their speech. I could also detect their lack of enjoyment of their job.

The cause of this lack of focus could certainly be debated. Whether it was due to an overwhelming agenda they could not wrap their arms around, or an inability to leave it, I could not say. I can say, without hesitation, that the distribution of their focus was most likely not balanced. They had become consumed by one focus. Could I have been meeting with a lot of people who were experiencing burnout? I believe most definitely so! Even though

I might have experienced this same thing during my career, I did not perceive it at the time.

What is never recognized during these periods of burnout is that it compromises productivity levels in all areas of one's life. Working more hours and having 24-hour worry does not necessarily equate to better results. A body drained of energy results in an energy-starved brain.

In an article titled "Be Smarter at Work, Slack Off," which appeared in *Fortune*, Ann Fisher quotes Professor Peter Capelli of management at Wharton as saying: "The physiological effects of tiredness are well-known. You can turn a smart person into an idiot just by overworking him." Health should always be a high priority because it affects so many areas of a person's life. Getting the proper amount of sleep is a major factor in a person's ability to achieve any objective. Bad health habits will always accelerate the "burnout" process.

In an article in the *Detroit Free Press* by Margarita Bauza, she quotes Michigan State University Labor & Industrial Relations researcher Ellen Kossek: "Burnout leads to accidents, arguments, breaks relationships and costs the bottom line."

Not being able to reduce stress and over-focusing in one area causes exhaustion, which makes one ineffective. Working on just one perceived priority is a human frailty that allows one focus to totally consume a person. It is only after a person leaves this situation entirely, that they realize the impact from single focus. The key is to always take a step back when you see this situation starting to evolve. Re-focus on balance. Focusing on priorities is an understandable agenda. However, when single-directed focus becomes all consuming, damage not only occurs in every area of your life, the benefit from this single focus is short-term, if any at all. Lack of balance can result in ineffectiveness everywhere.

The goal should be to do things in a way that will result in long-term gain. Long-term success comes from balance. With the long-term taken into consideration, you will be able to give your best to all areas of your life, including your job and yourself.

Let's look at a person whose scale of percentages is tilted heavily to the home area with little time for self or health. Work becomes a distraction that they make every effort to escape. Upon close observation, we might find this person having financial difficulties. This person possibly lives for today only.

The bottom line objective in any analysis of a person's focus should be diversification. Having a feeling of control and getting the most spice out of life requires participating actively in more than one area.

One of the worst things a person can do in life is to focus on one thing and shut out everything else, including one's self. This is a time bomb waiting to explode and destroy everything and anything in its path. History has documented some very successful people who dedicated and focused their lives on one thing or one goal. A close look also shows that some of those same people missed out on a lot of life as a result.

This should not be confused with the overused expression "keeping your eye on the ball." Focusing on an endeavor based on prioritized demands, within limits, is one thing. Focusing on one thing only and shutting out all other things and sacrificing relationships can result in abstract blindness.

If you don't give proper due to all of the things that matter, something will deteriorate, and ultimately affect all of the important things in your life. What you do at work affects what you do at home. What you do at home can affect what you do at work and what you do or don't do for yourself can affect both. If one area is not going particularly well, it impacts other areas because most people are limited in their ability to compartmentalize. "Things do not happen in a vacuum," as the old expression goes.

In my over thirty-five years in business, there is one phenomenon I have witnessed over and over again. This phenomenon is people basing their lives on one thing and giving little priority to anything else. The results, more often than not, produce chaos in all areas.

I worked with many people over the years who practiced little or no balance in their lives. In most cases, these individuals usually had tremendous difficulty in everything they did. It did not matter whether the imbalance was tilted to all work or to all home/self. The results were the same—lack of ownership, limited results, and lack of enjoyment in life.

For these individuals, there are always ongoing trials and tribulations that never seem to go away. With an off-kilter balance on focus, perspective becomes too narrow, and appreciation of responsibilities and others is severely impacted. There may be tremendous success in one area with one focus. However, you can bet that unwanted and unsuspected minefields are being planted in those ignored areas. Again, as a result, this success sometimes can be short-term. Always try to take work/life integration to the next level and not short change any facet of your life, and life's demands.

I can think of two people who worked for me over a significant period of time who fit this description. In order to keep the following two examples anonymous, we will refer to them as Mr. Doe and Ms. Doe.

Mr. Doe lived for his job because he could not seem to put together a life outside of work that brought him substance. Work was all that mattered to him, and so he immersed himself in his work. That was the appearance, at least on the surface. Everything he did was surface related, and others quickly recognized this trait in his personality. Relationships were only defined by what someone did for him or what they could do for him. He was not interested in bringing into his network anyone who could not in some way further his needs.

Mr. Doe made a point of surrounding himself with people he knew he could dominate. Those he could not dominate, he made every effort to undermine, especially those holding a position he wanted. He was also a bandwagon initiator; he either over-promoted a person's contribution or under promoted a person's contribution. Reality was never allowed to interfere with what might impact his business status. Since his world centered on him, his perspective was limited. It would not be an exaggeration to say that he was neither trusted nor liked by many outside this limited and ever-changing circle. In terms of being respected—no one respected him whether they were in his circle or not.

This approach to business and life outside of business was based on his inability to achieve any kind of balance in his life. The chicken or the egg analogy certainly could be a relevant question with regard to his plight.

He was a good example of how lack of balance in life can create an uncomfortable persona, limit focus, and result in limited enjoyment of the varieties of life. Variety is what creates full perspective. He had no desire in creating any kind of interest in anyone or anything outside of what impacted his work image.

He found it difficult to sustain any kind of long-term relationship or relationship of substance. The only things that mattered to him were appearance and how that appearance might impact his sense of authority. It goes without saying that title and position were important to him. He made it obvious.

Over the years that I worked with this person, I noted some common events that perpetually occurred. To sum it up, every-thing was always dramatic. He was rarely happy with anything outside of the work environment. He was not very creative because he limited his exposure to new ideas, thoughts, and individuals who might have more to offer other than their impact on his self-interest.

If I were to sum up this person's focus, I would say 100% of his focus was between work and himself. It was hard to separate the two in terms of how he functioned; they were really one and the same.

He constantly suffered from burnout. Balance and variety

could have done wonders for him, but the cycle had been set in motion. With this narrow perspective, the cycle just perpetuated itself.

Ms. Doe was the extreme opposite of Mr. Doe except for two similarities: they both lacked real confidence and they were both extremely insecure.

Ms. Doe was a likeable person, but her job meant little to her. Work was just a place she had to go to in order to receive a paycheck. The effort she was willing to give was limited; it was considered a major distraction to her outside life.

The little amount of professional respect she was given by peers directly correlated to the lack of quality work she contributed and her lack of devotion to responsibilities. She was respected as a person because deep down she was a good human being. She cared for her family. That made her a person of substance. She had no circle. Her future work prospects were limited because work was not important to her. The quality of work she produced also reflected that.

She was not a threat to anyone, and there was no circle for her because she had not created one. If she had made an effort to create a circle, no one would have felt compelled to join. There would be no gain. She was always accessible. Unfortunately, nobody much cared that she was accessible.

Mr. Doe and Ms. Doe did have one other thing in common. Ms. Doe, like Mr. Doe, did not create any kind of balance in her life. Ms. Doe's limited focus was her family. Unquestionably it is a great quality to live for one's family. However, Ms. Doe might have been able to contribute more to the well-being of her family if she had made an effort with her work responsibilities beyond just showing up.

Work was all that mattered to Mr. Doe. With little interest or responsibility outside of work, his home life was limited. For Mr. Doe, everything but work was nothing more than a potential adversary. Sadly, this perspective and approach to life resulted in him having many adversaries beyond what he may have really wanted.

Work mattered little to Ms. Doe. Her job was nothing more than a major adversary that got in the way of the other areas of her life. Sadly, this perspective and approach to life resulted in lack of success in many areas of her life.

Having balance in life means being as productive as you can be in every phase of life—work, home, and self. The gain from the same compartmentalized effort in all areas of a person's life is enjoyment and a full perspective. All areas, when given the same effort and substance, improve a person's chances for enjoyment in all areas. The parts together are what make for a healthy whole.

Focusing when at the job allows for enhanced quality time at home. Focusing on the moment at home allows you to give proper focus when at work. Having some time for you helps you appreciate yourself. It also allows you to direct your focus to work and home at the time each demands your focus. This is the way to reduce the adversary relationship of areas that many people have in their lives.

Work, home, health, and time for self should not be adversaries. The goal should be to give the proper focus to each as each demand while allowing them to work in harmony at the same time. The only way that happens is if each is not ignored during its time of need, and each is given the proper quality that each deserves. This is not a perfect world, so this process will not function as it should all of the time. Making an effort is the key here.

I would add that the importance of balance when adjusting to change in any area cannot be overstated. Balance is the second most important factor, second only to a positive perspective, when it comes to adjusting to change. I have managed through acquisitions, mergers, and restructuring and it was during these times when I noticed that the most balanced employees were able to transition much more easily than the single-focused employees.

Employees who had more balance in their lives were better able to put the change into perspective. They were better at minimizing the impact because they had other areas just as important to them in their lives. When an individual's whole life is defined by one thing, the impact of change in that area is significantly magnified. When work is recognized as only one facet of your life, you don't see yourself as wholly defined by it.

I have a saying that illustrates how to get the most out of every area in your life and be very productive: "Wherever you are, be there." The point is that you give your all to whatever you are doing at the moment. By totally focusing on where you are at a given moment, your chances of success are improved. Most importantly, when it is time to move on, you will be able to leave what you were doing.

Through execution of this perspective, distractions aren't so easily allowed to affect one's immediate focus. An example that any parent can easily identify with is when an enjoyable moment with a child is suddenly taken away by a work-related distraction. These precious times, when interrupted, create major parental guilt. Worse yet, being specific moments in time, they are gone forever. This moment that could have been so beneficial to both parent and child is gone. It can never be given back. Giving full attention to an unresolved work issue when it was the focus might have allowed this playtime to be playtime.

A saying that most people might feel has been overused for many years is "work smart." What does "work smart" mean? Working smart is another form of "wherever you are; be there." How are they the same?

The simple answer is that in order to work smart, you must acknowledge the importance of time and time management. In order to work smart, you must be efficient with your time and focus on the task in front of you. You cannot allow any distractions to take you away from your focus. This means utilizing your time well. Both sayings apply to the same principle. The only difference may be one saying we relate to home and the other we relate to work. Work and home can overlap, and so can these two principles.

One of the most important criteria I use to evaluate prospective employees is a person's perspective on balance. Integrity and character are also very important criteria. I have always believed that 80% of the people who applied for a position had the necessary skills. As such, an understanding of balance, integrity, and character become the most important attributes I look for when interviewing. Unlike integrity and character, balance can be learned.

As a general manager, I have never measured a person's contribution to my business based on the number of hours they worked. What I demand is focus, dedication, ownership, and good productivity that can only come from quality hours—not quantity of hours. My hope was that they would give the same in their personal lives. As a leader of an organization, it has always been important to me to promote the importance of home as much as the importance of the job.

I want my employees to work smart by functioning under the principle that wherever they are at the moment, they are there, not just physically but also mentally, emotionally, and spiritually. In the 21st century where there is no longer a line between home, work, and self, effective work/life integration is more important than it has ever been. It is the only way to achieve a form of balance one can live with.

The Balancing Act

Work	Home	Self/Health
1/3	*1/3*	*1/3*
Focus when there	**Enjoy the moments**	**Don't forget self**
Actual time in office	Time with family	Exercise time
Virtual office time	Time with friends	Reading a book
Calls/emails outside office	Entertainment activities	Clubs/organizations
Projects outside office	Family/children activities	Sports
Career development	Family dinners/projects	Career development/New Career

Summary

Focusing in only one area can cause chaos in all areas.

All of the important things in your life feed off of each other.

What affects you at work affects you at home.

What affects you at home affects you at work.

There should not be an adversarial relationship between work and home.

Understand your current focus distribution, and then form a plan.

Set daily goals in all areas.

Set annual and long-term goals, and make others aware of them.

"Wherever you are, be there."

Chapter 4

Have a Superior Work Ethic

Make work ethic an expectation you have of yourself

There are many who believe that we have seen the loss of work ethic over the last two decades. Even though many believe a good work ethic is an important trait, many also believe it is not practiced enough today.

The reason many people strive for a good work ethic is not what I believe it should be. Too many people in business use a good work ethic as a means to an end as opposed to an expectation they have of themselves.

I define "good work ethic" as focusing on quality productivity. This means utilizing your time well. It means having integrity and holding yourself accountable. This approach results in one achieving success over the long haul. **Having a superior work ethic is the third Way to Take Control of Your Destiny in Business and Life.**

I believe there are two issues in today's social environment that have had a significant impact on the effort most employees put into their work. The first issue revolves around the lack of balance between work and home that most employees struggle with. There is no longer a way to achieve a perfect balance because work demands and technology have erased time separations. We are again really talking about proper work/life integration as the goal.

As discussed in the chapter on balance, feeling stretched to the limit by both work and home results in compromised focus and compromised productivity in every area. This is by no means an excuse for going through the motions due to frustration.

The second issue affecting the effort people now give to their work responsibilities is a diminishing sense of loyalty to their employer. There is the mindset today that what we do as employees only benefits others. It does not improve any sense of security in one's own position. The problem with this perspective is that the basis for it is all wrong. As discussed in later chapters, we all really work for ourselves. A corporation only provides a vehicle for us to utilize our skills while compensating us for this effort. That effort contributes to the results of the company. In very basic, raw terms, this is an arrangement between a risk taker and an individual who provides skills and labor to the risk taker.

When discussing corporations today, it is hard to ignore the scandals we have witnessed when talking about ethics. There is no perfect definition of work ethics in this frame. The debate between the definition of business ethics, regulations, and corporate culture is a topic beyond this book. I will leave that long and complex debate for others.

In terms of the 15 Ways discussed in this book, ethics is measured in general by an individual's effort to a given task where he or she is being compensated by another. In terms of relating this to one's personal relationships, it is defined by the effort you give to a relationship.

Nothing is more upsetting than having an employee who spends more time and energy finding ways to get out of working than getting things done. Most people see work ethic directly correlated to employee loyalty. That only becomes correct if it is believed that good work habits benefit the employer only. I don't believe that is so; nor should it be. Good work ethics and productive work habits are as beneficial to employees as they are to the employer.

In a recent article on CNNMoney.com, senior writer Jeanne Sahadi gives the results of a survey released by *Salary.com and AOL*, a unit of Time Warner, on wasted time at work by the "typical American worker." The articles states: "More than 10,000 respondents in the online survey admitted to wasting, on average, 2.09 hours per day." In defining "wasted time," the article explains: "Their top time-wasting activities, they said, were making personal use of the Internet (including email), socializing with colleagues, conducting personal business, spacing out, running errands, making phone calls, applying for jobs, planning personal events, and arriving late or leaving early."

The article goes on to say that there is no difference in terms of gender. Men and women appear to waste time at work equally. Also introduced in this study is the theory that this so-called "wasting time" can actually be productive if it produces any form of creativity through non-work-related activity. Having some form of break time to recharge batteries and integrate other life responsibilities is important in today's work environment, be that environment brick and mortar or virtual. Where this integration consistently gets out of balance and work commitments suffer, we have a work ethic issue. Accountability applies to all, no matter what one's position is.

I believe it is possible to rationalize that some good can come from this non-work activity. However, I do not believe you can rationalize the whole 2.09 hours away. Many people simply waste time at work due to lack of interest. Lack of interest is just another justification for lack of work ethic. If you do not make an effort to manage your time well, you are not only cheating your employer, you are cheating yourself. In order to get the most out of anything you do, you must have a proactive perspective on what you do. People who feel good about what they do, make it their daily objective to get things done.

In terms of the contribution one gives in a personal relationship, the same criterion exists and applies. Most would agree that in order for a relationship to develop and grow, there must be a sincere, dedicated effort on the part of both individuals. An inconsistent or uninterested effort on the part of either individual in a relationship kills the relationship, period. No one person can be the contributor while the other just the receiver in any sustaining relationship. One person can be more congenial than another in a relationship. However, a situation where one person gives and the other makes little effort eventually kills the relationship.

People who have a positive outlook on life find joy in what they do. People who have a positive outlook in their personal relationships, find joy in nurturing those relationships. Be a happy worker. It will make anything you do more enjoyable, and people will enjoy being around you. Appreciate your personal relationships. You will not only get more in return, the relationship will develop and grow.

Even though it is understood that we cannot feel good and energized every day, work ethic does not need to be abandoned during those down days. Work ethic is a characteristic that defines you and lives with you throughout your career. Believe it or not, it is your signature; it is one way others define you.

Having stated that, I would add that nobody should ever completely define themselves by their job. A job is only a small window in defining who you are. However, your business peers most often view you according to what you bring to the business. Whatever that image is, it is hard to shake, be it bad or good.

The Work Ethic Execution

Your Gain	Employer Gain
Creates enjoyment	Creates appreciation
Exceed expectations	Expectation achieved
Consistency	Fills needs
Defines you	Perception defined
Impacts success of individual	Impacts success of company

Summary

Make work ethic an expectation you have of yourself.

Do things the way they should be done; results will follow.

Good work ethic is not something you do most of the time; it is something you do all of the time.

Your work ethic defines, in part, who you are.

Chapter 5

Embrace Integrity

Your judge and your jury is the mirror you look into
at the end of the day

Integrity is a term that has been so loosely tossed around it has not been given the respect it deserves. Many people describe themselves using this term because it has a good ring to it and it is recognized as a good thing.

Unfortunately, using it to describe oneself is one thing and following through in practice is another. We are challenged daily to release any grip it may have on us.

My definition of *integrity* simply comes down to trying to do the right thing at all times and treating others honestly and fairly.

Treating others fairly and being honest in today's extremely competitive world is a challenging task. It may seem as though you are compromising yourself at times when you carry this through. **Embracing integrity is the fourth Way to Take Control of Your Destiny in Business and Life.**

Doing the right thing and being honest with others also means making a judgment between what is right and what is wrong. It means looking at the big picture and weighing self-interest versus potential harm to others in the path. It means adhering to high principles when it is the most uncomfortable thing to do. Integrity not only enhances collaboration, it goes a long way in improving the world we work in.

Realistically, there are times beyond our control when we have to compromise our principles. For many reasons, beyond our control, we have no other choice. Our work responsibilities may dictate that we compromise our principles, at certain times. We still always have the ability to be honest and compassionate in this situation to lessen the impact. Nobody can ever take away your honesty or compassion, no matter what the situation.

As a general manager, I had to terminate or lay off employees because they could not carry out their responsibilities effectively. I have also had to terminate people due to a directive from higher-ups. Showing some compassion goes a long way for both parties in this situation. Whether one is on the receiving end or delivering the news, there is no perfect way to work through this process.

I have always tried to help others see that this was not a one-sided situation. In most cases, if the position is not a good fit for an individual, it is a problem for both parties. As a general manager or department head, being available in some way to help them transition to a better fit, when and where you can, can be good for both parties. Intent and results in this process sometimes do not match. You cannot be helpful to someone who does not want your help.

There was a time when I tried to help a sales manager I terminated transition to another company and it backfired on me. I would still do it again. I made a call on his behalf and helped him get an interview after I terminated him. The recommendation I had given was an honest assessment. I believed that a different environment and a fresh start, based on what he had hopefully learned, would benefit both him and the new employer.

Unfortunately, his difficulty working with my experienced sales staff was not his only problem. His difficulty was that he was not open to new ideas and approaches to issues. This is a problem that can transcend employers, no matter the environment. Unfortunately, the new job I helped him get did not work out. I was disappointed it did not work out. After all, I had called and recommended him to this new employer.

I have also seen many times where a promotion was so important to a person that he or she would do anything to make others look bad in order to elevate his or her own status for the position. This same person usually was quite fickle in his relationships with coworkers and subordinates. This pattern was not hard to decipher. This person lacked integrity and everyone that came in contact with him figured it out quickly.

We have all interacted with these people. They appear to always get ahead and stay in front of others by using ruthlessness, deceit, unethical lying, and cheating as a functional skillset. If you look a little closer and watch long enough you might be surprised at where this skillset takes this person.

Eventually, this lack of authenticity does catch up to them. There are many problems and challenges in this dysfunctional mode of operation. In general, these kinds of actions require tremendous acting. The perpetual by-products of this acting are where the real issues surface.

Jack Welch, ex-CEO of General Electric and "manager of the 20th Century" mentions in his book *Winning* that authenticity was one of the most important characteristics he looked for when hiring executives. His basis for the importance of authenticity is that in order for people to follow someone, a person must believe that person is real. They must be who they appear to be. That leader must be comfortable with who they are.

When Jack Welch talks about authenticity he is really talking about an inner core of integrity and honesty. If you are authentic, you are honest with others. You don't communicate to others just what you think they want to hear.

I believe that authenticity is not only an important characteristic for leaders; it is also important in any communication.

Integrity allows a person to accept themselves for who they are. It allows for sincere and direct communication. This is how things get done over the long-term. This is how relationships continue over the long haul and survive obstacles, challenges, and distractions.

Integrity eliminates the need to peel through layers to get to the truth, a process that leaves the receiver tired and eventually disinterested. Having integrity helps you be more productive by reducing wasted resources, getting to the root of issues.

It is important to understand that life is a marathon, not a short race. The key to enjoyment of any long-term success, business or personal, is to know you gave your best and tried to do things the right way. You can't expect to be ahead at every turn or win every race, but you should expect to give your best in every race.

The test at the end of the day is simple. Be able to look in the mirror and feel good about what you see. You answer to yourself first. If you can feel good about what you have done and know you have given your best, then it has been a successful day, no matter the results.

We live in a world where people have shied away from accountability; my generation created the foundation of that concept. We fought the institutional and traditional thought of the generation before us. They believed judging right from wrong was not only right but that it was a given that did not warrant debate.

The baby boomers fought that mentality and replaced it with the belief that "if it feels good, do it" and "no one has the right to sit in judgment." If it works for me and adversely affects others, that is their problem, not mine. There is no principle of right and wrong other than what may be illegal. Do what is right for yourself, even if it may be at the expense of others.

The end result of this thinking is we have become a "me" world where not too many limitations exist. Questioning is limited by what may be considered "politically incorrect."

This new perspective initiated by my generation as a rebellion of previous social and institutional standards has now become the norm. Unfortunately, this "me" approach does not mesh well with integrity. Taking others into consideration may impact what we believe is most beneficial to us as individuals. Having integrity means you do care what others think. More importantly, it means being aware that what you do can affect others, either in a positive way or adversely.

This new "who cares?" perspective permeating society today has produced a world where there is limited trust. Over the long haul, this if-it-feels-good-and-it-is-right-for-me approach will not produce real self-actualization.

Not only is it possible to have integrity and be successful, it is still the best way to insure a feeling of success that you can live with.

Be a person people can trust. Minimize the compromising of your principles. But, where you have to do something that compromises those principles, incorporate honesty, hope, and fairness as much as you can into the mix.

Summary

Integrity is not only the way to long-term success; it is the way to insure a success you can live with in the long-term.

Be a person others can trust.

Life is a marathon; give your best for the long haul.

Chapter 6

Take Ownership

As long as you feel you work for someone else, your effort is compromised

If you ask people who they work for, it is safe to say that 99% of them would give a name of a company. If you believe that you only work for a person or an entity, and that everything you do is solely for that entity, the effort you give is compromised.

With this compromised perspective, there is the belief that any effort just furthers an entity's or another person's agenda. Nothing is further from the truth. Everything you do defines you as a business contributor, as a worker, and as a person. **Taking ownership is the fifth Way to Take Control of Your Destiny in Business and Life.**

There are two tremendous by-products of any involvement in a work-related responsibility or a personal responsibility. The first by-product from a fully involved effort is individual development derived from that endeavor. The second is the contribution a fully involved effort makes to your long-term marketability.

When you take complete ownership of an effort, ability to learn from that endeavor is enhanced proportionately. You pay more attention to detail and the process and, as a result, are in a better position to learn from the experience. You learn what it takes to get through the process, what has worked, and what has not. This puts you in a better position to apply it in the future. You have eliminated the worst enemy of business and individuals: falling into a mechanical process.

A *mechanical process* means you are just going through the motions. You are operating with a blindfold on. This is how businesses and individuals arrive at a certain point with no understanding of how they got there. The end result of this chaos is future repetition. History repeats itself.

The enhanced marketability derived from taking ownership also creates a better chance for enhanced success. By taking ownership, results are more often than not more successful. Learning along the way means that marketability to your current employer and a future employer is increased dramatically. The demand for what you can do tomorrow and in the future goes to another level. This is basic economics.

Taking ownership is not only beneficial to your employer—it is extremely beneficial to you. There are times during a career when an incompetent manager may make you feel detached and diminish your motivation. This feeling could result from an unexplained compensation package change or the elimination of what was a long-term benefit. Another example of this de-motivation may be a manager allowing demeaning interaction that creates a miserable work environment.

There are too many managers who are clueless about employee motivation and how to create loyalty. Nor do they care to learn. The reality is that you become your own motivator. This is where your motivation should be rooted anyway. This really is your responsibility; it should not be totally the responsibility of your employer.

Business management philosophies change over the course of decades. Unfortunately they can fluctuate between employee friendly and non-employee friendly. This ridiculous fluctuation does not exist in aware and progressive companies. It has been proven that autocratic management does not work over the long haul for most companies, especially today.

Most recently we have seen more inclusive environments in today's business world. Google is a good example of this inclusive environment. This approach is based on an under-standing that employee well-being and decision involvement can have a beneficial impact on the results of the business. Employees today seek a mentor more than a boss. Being a mentor takes leadership. Position should not define the level of buy-in one has relative to responsibilities and ownership.

Bottom line, no matter what the environment is, the best way for an individual to achieve results, both short-term and long-term, is by taking ownership.

By taking ownership, you are able to maximize work enjoyment and expand your skillset. The key, within reason, is to be able to work in and through any management style that your supervisor subscribes to. By taking ownership, you will be able to work through any economic or specific business cycle. Taking ownership is what shields you or insulates you from any outside actions on the part of others. Happenings outside of your individual ownership environment lose significance and impact. It allows you to feel good about what you do regardless of the negative actions of others.

This also applies to personal relationships. When you take ownership of what you provide to a relationship on a daily basis, it creates a foundation for growth. It also can motivate the receiver to take the same ownership.

A few years ago I worked with a vice president who defined this give-and-take in a relationship in a succinct way. She had taken it from Stephen Covey's *The Seven Habits of Highly Successful People*. The premise bases interaction in a relationship as being defined as either deposits or withdrawals. Again, it can apply to personal relationships as well as business relationships. A deposit is a feel-good interaction. A withdrawal may be when actions taken may reduce one's self-esteem. At the end of the day, everyone wants to have more deposits than withdrawals. Defining Covey's definition this way does label interactions in a plus or minus format. It also becomes something a person can do for him or herself.

A deposit can be a thank you for a job well done while a

withdrawal can be verbal feedback on a task that did not go well. By taking ownership of who you are and what you do, you can impact the balance of your account while others are making their deposits and withdrawals. I believe that through our perspective, we impact that balance in our account at the end of the day.

There is another way to look at ownership when it comes to business and our personal lives. There are three important factors that measure our net worth to a business or a relationship. They are our ability and effort to nurture and build the relationship, our contribution to the value of the relationship, and our marketability. Marketability refers to the overall value we bring today and tomorrow.

Taking ownership impacts all of these factors significantly. Taking ownership as opposed to just taking what comes enhances your chances of producing better results. Take ownership; it is a responsibility you owe yourself.

The Ownership Option

Ownership Approach Work for self:	Non-Ownership Perspective You work for others:
Increases effort	Compromises effort
Defines a person	It's a job
Improves perspective	Limits perspective
Improves marketability	Limits options
Eliminates "going through the motions"	Creates a "going through the motions"
Creates self-motivation	Need to be motivated by others
Works through economic/management cycles	Uncomfortable with change

Summary
Everything you do defines you as a contributor, worker, and

person.

As long as you feel you work for someone else, your effort is compromised.

Taking ownership improves perspective, learning, and marketability.

Taking ownership may be a benefit to an employer, but it is a huge benefit to an individual.

Take control over your own motivation.

Chapter 7

Don't Burn Bridges

Continually maintain and build your network

Over the course of a career, people voluntarily or involuntarily change employers about nine times, if not more often. At the moment of termination, it is human nature to lay on the line all repressed ill will felt over the years working for that employer.

It may seem like a good time to release repressed dislike for a manager to the manager's supervisor as a payback. The reality is that what you say under these circumstances will most likely have little impact. The reason is you are leaving and the person in question is still in place. That fact alone eliminates any leverage there may be in what you have to offer, or any credibility in what you say. This does not mean that companies do not want feedback; they do. Many companies give exit interviews, but the reality is, exit interviews carry little weight. This is especially true if the employee is being terminated.

Companies are like clubs. Nobody wants to hear something negative about a club they are still emotionally and financially attached to. The best you can do is offer, in positive terms, your view of potential issues along with believed solutions based on your experience. Again, this should be conveyed in the most positive terms. They are then given a choice to consider what you have provided or ignore it altogether.

The worst thing to do is go through an emotional release of all that you have repressed and have it come out like an atomic explosion. You will merely be looked at as emotionally disturbed at best. At worst, it becomes a bridge that has been destroyed and a reference that has been compromised.

Not burning bridges is the sixth Way to Take Control of

Your Destiny in Business and Life. Burning bridges does not just apply to separation between an employee and employer. It also applies to business relationships and personal relationships. In order to get the most out of life in every area and increase your ability to succeed going forward, every bridge must be open. That is how you add to your network over a lifetime, as opposed to subtracting from it.

Every person that you come in contact with, in business or personally, may be a potential contributor to your future well-being and success. That makes every person you interact with a potential beneficial resource.

With this perspective, you are more appreciative of people you meet in any setting. You are better able to enjoy others for who they are as opposed to how they may appear to impact you at the moment. This perspective also allows you to bond with people who otherwise would not have been allowed past your "firewall." As Yogi Berra might say, "You never know what you may have missed out on, because you missed out on it."

It is natural to give little attention to people you meet on a daily basis. Everyone is so busy; we are always moving on to the next thing. It is worth taking the time to give these interactions some quality.

Let's look at some examples of interactions we take for granted. First and foremost on this list is the supervisor you report to. You may work for someone who you don't particularly like and who you consider to be difficult to report to.

Consider for a minute the possibilities as to why this individual may be so difficult to work for. It could be that he or she does not interact well with others and has no idea how to motivate people. You might believe this person should not hold this position, but it is also possible this individual fits the company culture well.

If this person is a natural fit for the company culture and you dislike the environment, you may be in the wrong company. Your ability to utilize and enhance your skillset in this company may be limited. If that is the case, so be it. However, there still may be important benefits you may be receiving in this situation. Your business relationships in this company may also be beneficial. Given all these variables, both pro and con, it could make sense for you to look outward for another position. But understand that you are the one defining this situation as not viable. Leaving with a good relationship in place with this supervisor may still make sense.

The new company where you are applying will not contact your current employer for a reference because you still are employed there. However, consider that you may, at some point, leave this new employer in the future. Guess who the employer they call now becomes? It is also not uncommon for supervisors to give an off-the-record summary of a former employee who worked for them. At some point in our career, we all work for people who may be difficult to report to. You not only can learn from these individuals, you may cross paths with them again. They may surface as a future coworker, a future client, or an unsuspecting reference you did not request nor expect.

People lose prospective jobs, clients, and opportunities every day because they did not have the foresight to keep a relationship intact. I can come up with two specific examples where I benefited from retaining a good working relationship that I could have easily damaged at an earlier date. I took the high road, and it paid dividends.

As a general manager in wireless, I had been working with a hotel (I will leave unnamed), where I had an excellent working relationship with the general manager. This relationship was developed through us working together to put a tower on his business's building. We teamed up in a golf league which further enhanced the business relationship. Unfortunately, at a later time, his corporation moved him to another hotel in another state. He was replaced by another general manager who did not approve of the business agreement our two businesses had created. Continuing this business relationship became challenging. Needless to say, we lost some business from this client. I kept the relationship as respectful as it had been when my golfing buddy was running the hotel. Ten years later, this general manager, who was now at a different hotel, was a prospective client of my new consulting firm.

In the 1980s, I worked for a corporation that owned many television stations, radio stations, and outboard advertising operations around the country. I lost my position when the company brought in an individual and positioned him to buy the station. I lost my job because the new owner also served as his own general manager. In addition, I lost thousands of dollars due to a technicality in my non-compete with the company. I could have easily sued and made this a nasty situation. I did not. I agreed to a reasonable settlement while doing everything I could to maintain a good, ongoing, respectful relationship. In the long run, because of my desire to keep this relationship intact, I actually came out significantly further ahead financially.

My payback came ten years later, when I was interviewing for a general manager position with the chairman and president of a wireless company in New Jersey. Oddly enough, the president of the broadcasting company and the chairman of the wireless company were next-door neighbors in Florida. These were two individuals whose primary residences were in two different parts of the country. It was fairly easy for them to get together to discuss my credentials. I did get hired by the wireless company, helped by a glowing report from the president of the company I worked for ten years earlier.

My current position is a perfect example of future gains from not burning bridges. I currently serve as the chief operating officer/executive vice-president of a company that I left over thirty years ago. I kept this bridge open for many years while serving as general manager for many different companies. I never had plans to come back, but I always kept the bridge intact.

I could give many more examples of relationships kept intact that paid dividends in the future. I will summarize this by stating my beneficial contacts continue to include past associates, past peers, and past employees. Many positive business transactions have occurred as a result, and continue to occur, because these contact relationships are intact.

How important is it to also strive to keep a good relationship with customers or clients that you meet in person or over the phone? It is just as important to keep these relationships intact as it is with supervisors and coworkers. The examples given above also can occur with clients and customers. A past customer can always become a potential future customer. That customer may even become a future prospective employer. It is not only a small world; it is getting smaller every day!

Do you think this same approach should be considered when it comes to personal acquaintances? Yes, most definitely. The same examples that were given for supervisors, coworkers, and customers apply to any person you come in contact with in your personal life.

How many people do you think get confrontational on the road, or display the international symbol of disdain in a dispute with another driver? It is very possible repercussions unknowingly have occurred at a later date from something that simple. Have you ever walked into a meeting and been introduced to someone who looked familiar and you did not know why? The only hope you can have is that the interaction in the past was a good one. Have you ever walked into a meeting and been introduced to someone you previously had a bad interaction with? At that point, you knew the outcome of the meeting included obstacles you had not considered in your preparation.

Make every attempt to create good closure in any interaction with another, whether you like them or not. You never know when you may have to cross that bridge again. It is difficult to cross a bridge that you happened to blow up years earlier. Continually adding to your network will increase the size of your infrastructure. Nurturing it will keep it intact. Being intact is the starting point to perpetual growth and expansion. That is the kind of impact you want in the long-term.

The Bridge-Building Box

Build	**Burn**
Adds to network	Limits network
Every new relationship is an opportunity	Relationships as a necessity
At break, leave with mutual respect	At break, breaks relationship
Every job an opportunity to add	Every job stands alone

Summary

When you make a change in life, don't close bridges or damage relationships that took time to build.

Always try to leave any interactive relationship with mutual respect.

Learn and consider every job or position an opportunity to gain something you will use at a later date.

Chapter 8

Security Comes From Within

You are the CEO of your own Company

There has always been an unwritten rule of business that an employee's job security is directly related to that person's contribution to the profitability of the company. Certainly, being a good contributor does definitely keep one in good favor with their employer. However, this is nothing more than surface security. Real security comes from oneself and is not something someone can give to you.

Anyone who has been in the business world over ten years realizes that economic cycles and a company's success are what determine the length of this false security. The truth is that basing your security on factors and people you have little control over is a tenuous way to define your security. **Recognizing that security comes from within is the seventh Way to Take Control of Your Destiny in Business and Life.**

No matter your position, management or staff, handing off that responsibility to another, always creates a potentially precarious foundation. Companies get caught up in cycles tied to the economy of the day. And, in this ever-changing competitive business world, companies get caught up in short-term planning. Today's objectives become today's priorities. There are an infinite number of examples that support this. In earlier years, before major mergers, acquisitions, and the extinction of mom-and-pop businesses, the business climate was different. This major consolidation in many industries began in earnest around the early 1990s and has not slowed down.

Unfortunately, too many companies today live and breathe with a short-term objective mentality. As a result, they become susceptible to changing business and economic environments. They limit their adaptability and, worse yet, function in a reactionary mode instead of a proactive one.

All that you can achieve by tying your security to this kind of ship is the chance that when high tide sets in, you could experience a rough and bumpy ride at best. The best course you can follow is to take responsibility for steering your own dinghy while helping the big ship move forward.

There are many examples of companies that have experienced dramatic changes that have affected the security of many people. Enron is one such company. The Enron scandal was far-reaching and impacting. Many employees not only lost their jobs, they lost future retirement investments that included investments in the company. They were really "all in."

This does not mean that you should not trust the company you work for. It accentuates the importance of being your own advocate. Perpetually take a step back and evaluate your situation as objectively as possible. Entertain the what-ifs.

You should make sure you are consistently contributing to the success of your employer. At the same time, you also need to keep a close eye on your own success at all times. At the end of the day, we are all individual companies that have individual financial responsibilities. You own your future, and you should continually prepare for that future.

Early in my career, I worked for a few companies that I was sure I would retire from. In fact, I felt this way about the first company I worked for after graduating from college. Although not on the national magnitude of an Enron, this national company woke up one day and realized it could no longer compete. Changes in the law had affected its ability to compete. Bad planning created an inability to adjust. The dynamics in the business environment had changed. The company had not. Many long-time employees suddenly found themselves in a restructuring nightmare.

There can always be some gain in riding out a bumpy ride, especially if you are recognized as a major contributor who is trying to advance in the company. Also, not every company that finds itself in a competitive, financial, or scandalous crisis ends up going out of business.

It is during these major business or industry challenging cycles that you must really maximize your contribution. Your ability to persevere and even grow during rough times is not overlooked by most company executives. In addition, individual growth during crisis times is when leaders are born. Every person in a business is valued and rated based on the return they provide for the company on its investment. You would look at this the same way if you carried the responsibility and risk as an owner or shareholder. It is unfortunately a fact of business. It is important to understand that even though difficult transitions produce individual pain, they also can provide a great opportunity for learning and career gain.

The pain is why most people use the terms *stress* and *overworked* when discussing their jobs. We have been in this latest cost-cutting cycle since early 2000. I'm not sure too many "experts" expected we would still be in that mode in 2015. We have seen this cycle a few times in the last forty years. The early 1970s, early 1980s, and early 1990s saw periods of heavy cost cutting and restructuring in business. History has shown that these challenging economic times will continue to surface on a cyclical basis.

Being overworked is usually a by-product of the cost-cutting demands resulting from over-budgeted revenues. Most businesses answer to banks, investors, and shareholders, and in many cases to all three. Meeting a certain profit margin becomes more than just a goal. Expenses have been budgeted based on reaching those revenues, and if the revenue does not come in, something has to give.

If you see your security being dependent on other people's

decisions, your by-product is worry. That leaves little time to spend evaluating the most important development process. That development process is what you provide yourself on a daily basis! The reality is that when you grow and develop as a contributor, you win and the company wins. It is a win-win situation.

We hear so often the term *politics* used by a person knowingly or unknowingly defining their sense of security in the company they work for. Everyone at one time or another has made the statement that they are tired of all the politics in their business. The underlying message here is that they are not comfortable with their relationships with the "right people."

As much as politics should not be a factor in determining who is in good standing, too many companies accept this kind of culture. It's human nature. The individual who is not in the "circle" should not want his or her security defined by others who happen to be in the "circle."

It is the unknown—"what is going to become of me"—that really causes this tremendous feeling of lack of control and insecurity. The unknown is the thing that most people cannot handle. That is why when a person leaves a company or is asked to leave a company there can be a sudden rush of relief. For a moment in time, the politics or the unknown status has been defined. It may be a good outcome, where a person leaves voluntarily for another position. It may be the relief from closure to a bad situation, even where a person has been involuntarily terminated.

There is another related stress created by a person tying his or her security to another person's evaluation of their contribution. When we rely on others to provide this security, our own self-development and growth is ignored. Worse yet, our marketability for other positions, increased responsibility in our current company, or potential future positions in other companies may be missed as a result.

Your marketability with your current company and any future endeavor is directly related to your individual growth. If you, like any product, have expanded your value, marketing yourself will be easy. This is economics at its simplest.

Don't waste valuable time stressing about the control others have on your present and future, when the real control is in your hands.

When you view yourself as a product, and recognize that you are the chairman, president, and CEO of your own company, you know you control your destiny. This perspective allows you to focus more on doing something to constantly evaluate and improve yourself. Less time is wasted on worrying about the control you think others may have on your livelihood. This perspective allows you to continually develop many options.

You are the chairman. You are the president. You are the CEO. You own your own company. You subcontract your skills, abilities, and knowledge to formal institutions. Take care of it, grow it, and market it on a perpetual basis.

Granted, some companies may misuse your company. The reality is that not all companies and managers are competent. It is one reason why some companies go out of business. This under-use is caused by managers who don't understand skillsets and have little ability in developing employees. Not all managers are good at skillset analysis, or efficient in training and mentoring others. Sometimes companies also don't do a good job matching skillsets to positions.

No matter how you define security or pursue it, its root has to come from within. When there is an understanding that security is something that is self-rooted, it becomes easier to achieve and maintain over the long haul. That person now has control over providing it.

Commit to perpetual development. Commit to perpetual learning. Dedicate yourself to always adding to the attributes, skills, knowledge, and ability that you bring to any situation.

This mission is what will perpetually enhance your marketability. This marketability applies to your present environment and your future environment.

Keep your options open, and remember there is no such thing as just luck. You make your own luck. Luck is nothing more than preparing for opportunities that may present themselves. Contrary to what many people believe, luck comes from a lot of hard work and dedicated effort. Luck at its most raw definition is created through a security-from-within perspective.

The Security Circle

Takes Responsibility/Manages Self

Self-Development　　　　　　*Sense of Control*
Career Development　　　　　CEO of Self-Company

SECURITY

Constantly Improves　　　　*Comfortable with Change*
Marketability　　　　　　　Dedication/Passion
Sees Opportunity　　　　　　Takes Risks

Summary
Look at yourself as a perpetually developing product.
You are the president of your own company.
You are the CEO of your own company.
You are the chairman of your own company.

Chapter 9

Be a Visionary

Without a vision, there is no target

Anyone who ever achieved a long-term goal will tell you it started with a vision. You have to visualize something first for it to happen. Visualizing gives you a tangible target. You must first know where you want to go before a road map can be created. **Having a vision is the eighth Way to Take Control of Your Destiny in Business and Life.**

Companies continually talk about visions and mission statements and goals. The problem is that all they really ever do is just talk about it. Many never take the time to set the goals that are necessary to achieve it. Worse yet, and most importantly, some never convey it to employees.

In general, we may perceive our employers' purpose. However, as employees, we interpret how that relates to our individual responsibilities. You could call this *territorial vision*, because it is limited to our individual functions. As an example, an employee in a restaurant, given no company vision, functions on the basic premise that the restaurant is there to sell meals. If they are a waitperson, their job is to serve the meals. Without any company vision, the waitperson's job is simply defined as serving meals, period. As such, all of the waitpersons do their basic job, yet probably perform at different levels based on individual skills and ownership of those responsibilities. Unfortunately, this may mean the same objective is not necessarily shared by everyone in the company. Everybody is doing their own thing. If this restaurant has a vision, understood by all employees, of providing the best customer service in the region, we have an entirely different environment.

I have attended many company strategic-planning seminars for middle and upper management. Oddly enough, at one of these events, when we were asked what the company's vision was, the answer was consistent. Nobody had a clue. This was a group of general managers running the regions throughout the country for the company! The general managers had never had a long-term vision conveyed to us by the corporate executives we reported to. Our only mission, if honestly acknowledged, was to meet the current profitability goals, period. Beyond today, it was anyone's guess. Given the lack of a national vision, it was important for us as general managers to create our own vision. We had our budgets that we negotiated with corporate every year. Those numbers were a compromise between company demand and regional-based economy and other impacting variables.

But a budget is one thing; a vision is something altogether different. A vision is a long-term expectation. It is where you see yourself way down the road. Most often when we think of vision we think of Thomas Edison and the light bulb or Albert Einstein and the Theory of Relativity or Martin Luther King and equal opportunity for every person.

Achievement is dependent on vision. Vision is the common denominator for any success ever achieved. You cannot separate the two because things do not happen in a vacuum. There is always a start and there is always an end to everything. No company can be successful over the long haul without a vision, a mission, and continual goals in place. These goals must be flexible in order to meet business environmental changes that occur along the way. A company needs to be able to fine tune the strategic plan as unrealized or anticipated bumps occur. It is even possible for a vision to be significantly altered based on unanticipated events. But there must be a generally defined vision, understood by all employees. A simple vision may be for a company name to be synonymous with "elite customer service" or with the fastest Internet service available.

In formulating a vision for a company, there are many important variables that have to be taken into consideration. Because time does not stand still, the variables that affect the vision must have adaptability, an ability to be altered. Think about all of the communication changes we have seen in the last twenty-five years with the advancement of technology. Wireless and the Internet have dramatically impacted the way business professionals communicate and exchange data. The wireless technology and the Internet have also dramatically impacted the way we interact. Our ability to keep in contact on a daily basis is more than we ever could have imagined possible fifteen years ago. How many people communicate through letter writing today?

When you consider the significant elements that can impact the vision of a company, it is easy to conclude that formulating a vision can be a daunting task. Some of those elements are government regulations, population changes and shifts, the competitive mix, national policy, specific industry cycles and perpetually changing local and global economies.

Beginning a discussion about formulating a vision for a company is a lengthy subject. For our purposes, we will pick up the subject based on the premise that all of these complex variables have already been considered and the company has now promulgated its message in a viable form. The vision is in place and adaptable to any economic, sociological, demographic, technological, and global changes on the horizon.

The first point is that the vision has to be adaptable, yet understood by all, in order for it to come to fruition. It must be understood what those variables are today, how they may change in the future, and where the company is today and where it expects to be tomorrow. There must be a long-term plan in place, period. Without this vision and map, there is no purpose. If you don't know where you are going or where you want to go, you end up going where others happen to send you.

Not only does all this hold true for companies, it also applies to individuals. Companies must have a vision in order to be successful long-term. Individuals need their own vision. As individuals, we align our business goals to our specific responsibilities. However, position responsibilities, company structure, and company direction are always subject to change; some are announced and some just happen. Just as a company can go out of business, an individual can be taken out of a business or leave a business.

An individual with a vision allows for thinking beyond the company while contributing to the success of the company. By having an individual vision, a person can better focus on job responsibilities and productivity while promoting individual long-term success. This is again one of those win-win situations. Everyone benefits.

One of the most important benefits you receive from individual vision is the ability to work through work-related and personal rough situations. Add to this the resulting ability to take some emotion out of an event and think more logically. Answers suddenly come more easily, and an ability to cope is increased significantly.

A person who has the ability to see any rough situation as a means to an end or a necessary step in a process is better equipped to deal with it. Your view of an event takes on a different perspective.

Understand your company's vision, if there is one. Most importantly, make sure you have a business and personal vision of your own. Without a vision, you could aimlessly live day to day, taking only what life has to offer. This aimless approach becomes, at best, a going-through-the-motions endless cycle, and at worst, can produce a victim mentality. Purpose is important. We all define this in our own terms. Visions do not have to be complicated nor do they have to be tangible. A vision may be as simple as enjoying life to its fullest, appreciating interactions with others, appreciating loved ones, or an appreciation for the small things in life. That is a good vision, and one that helps you get through difficult times while looking forward to good times. It also can create good times.

Is it possible to have a vision of aimlessness with the mission being to live day to day and take life as it comes? Yes, technically that is a vision. It is a purpose. The bottom line is defining what makes you happy and having a perpetual plan to do your best to make that happen.

With aimlessness as a goal, putting current events into perspective might be a little more difficult because they no longer are defined as a means to an end. They would be business as usual and, as such, could be all-consuming.

Events and situations that become all-consuming, and they do happen whether you have a vision or not, can become exhausting and overwhelming. The purpose of a vision is not only to give you purpose; it is a means of reducing the magnitude of the event that happens today.

Having a vision is a major step in being able to see yourself beyond your employer and your personal relationships. Having a vision allows you to proactively detach yourself from rough business and personal events while allowing you to function effectively with a proactive perspective and appreciation.

Formulating a vision is not as difficult as it may seem. The first step to defining your vision is to understand what your business, financial, and personal situation is today. The next step, in very simple terms, is to determine what you would like that situation to look like tomorrow, months from now, and in the coming years.

Define the present and determine what you want the future to look like, whether we are talking about a month, a year, or years from now. Then define what the difference is between the two. You can now create the game plan.

Let's make up a simple example. Today you are single, working as an assistant manager for a company, and don't have the education you believe you need to advance in business nor do you feel confident in interacting with others.

Your vision is to be in a relationship, be in a manager's position, complete your degree, and feel confident about yourself. How do you get this done? The answer is to visualize what you want and formulate a game plan and a specific strategy that will complete the vision.

In our example, your anticipated completion of this vision should be given a target date. This vision should be adaptable to changes that occur in your life. Even though you are giving it a target date, a good vision is always an ever-evolving process.

These visions to become involved in a meaningful relationship, advance at work, and build your self-esteem need a mission-defined road map. This is how you make a vision become reality. The key to getting this done would be to get involved in activities geared to achieving that vision.

Finding that relationship you are looking for is a subjective process. The idea is to find ways that will increase your chances of meeting someone. Beyond that, I won't make any recommendations.

In order to be promoted to a manager position, you might dedicate yourself to working closely with the current manager to learn all you can. Take on more responsibilities that can help accelerate your training. Read articles, books, and listen to CDs that offer skill enhancement. Increase your knowledge and expertise of your industry. These are all self-initiated activities that can complement what you are already exposed to by your employer. When the opportunity presents itself, you will be ready.

In order to advance your educational background, take some classes at the local college with a target date in terms of getting a degree that could further your career opportunities.

It is important to have any vision be an all-encompassing one. A vision should take into consideration every area of your life while impacting each area.

Always have a vision of the future. At the same time, do all you can in the present to make that vision happen. It not only gives you a great feeling of control, it makes the road along the way much more enjoyable. It is also the best way to develop a taking-control-of-your-life perspective.

The Visionary Vertical

The Vision

B	P	
U	E	
S	R	
I	S	*The Mission Helps Achieve the Vision*
N	O	
E	N	
S	A	
S	L	*Strategic & Tactical Objectives Achieve Mission*

Summary

An individual vision allows you to work through difficult personal and business situations.

A vision enables you to take the emotion out of an event and see more clearly.

A vision gives you purpose.

Chapter 10

Like and Appreciate Yourself

Confident people are like magnets

Self-esteem is the most underrated and ignored issue there is when it comes to human relationships. The old saying that you must "first like yourself before others can like you" holds much truth.

A person's self-esteem is a major factor in how well one performs in any business or personal endeavor. When you feel good about yourself, you focus much more on a task and less on how you are viewed. Because we like ourselves, we believe others should feel the same. **Liking and appreciating yourself is the ninth Way to Take Control of Your Destiny in Business and Life.**

People spend too much time worrying about how they are viewed by others. This just adds more pressure and stress to any task or interaction with another individual.

I am not saying you should take this "like for oneself" to the stage of narcissism. However, having a positive image and self-respect allows you to enjoy your own company. It also allows you to take your interaction to another level. That higher level will enhance collaboration significantly.

An individual who appreciates who they are, short of being arrogant, radiates a vibrant aura of confidence that is felt by everyone they come in contact with. That self-appreciation also makes the individual fun to be around. That feel-good aura is also passed on to others through interaction. An individual, who for the most part is confident and feels good about himself, without being self-absorbed, can light up a room with his presence. He becomes a magnet.

When people have this confidence, they are better able to spend quality time with others. They can focus on getting to know others and enjoy people for who they are. They take the time to look beyond the surface. For most people, the real person is usually beyond the outer surface. Have you ever gotten to like someone who you did not like at that first introduction?

Anyone can learn to appreciate and like themselves. It's really the easiest thing to do if you are armed with a proper perspective. The first key to appreciating yourself is to start with the given that no one is perfect. We all make mistakes.

Making mistakes should not diminish how you feel about yourself or how others feel about you. Making mistakes is a common result for all of us at given points in time.

The second key to feeling good about yourself is to try to always learn from mistakes that you make. The goal is to eliminate repetition, and be more aware of the cause-and-effect relationship of decisions. Learning from your mistakes not only helps you deal with the results, it creates solutions and closure at the same time. Making progress in anything makes you feel good about yourself.

Thirdly, we all have some good attributes but we don't take enough time to recognize and enjoy them. People spend too much time focusing on the characteristics they don't have and wish they had. A simple example is someone who is extremely tall wishing they were shorter or someone who is not very tall wishing they were taller. These are two changes science is not capable of addressing. The best way to deal with any characteristic you have that you don't like is to either do something to change it, if it is changeable, or learn to deal with it and move on. Closure is what allows us to accept something we don't particularly like. Closure allows us to focus on those things we can impact.

Give proper attention to the things that you can impact. Impacting things that are important to you elevates self-esteem.

Proper focus can be the difference between perpetuating a self-defeating attitude and a proactive belief you can accomplish almost anything.

Why do people continually make the same mistakes over and over again while questioning the repetitive results? Why do some people take on a "why me?" perspective and believe they have no control over anything that happens to them? Why do some people perpetuate a feeling that nothing ever goes right?

All of these questions can be addressed with one statement: They do not like themselves as much as they should, and therefore do not wish to take responsibility for what happens to them. They would rather pass that responsibility onto another because they don't have the confidence in their own ability to get things done.

The end result of self-pity is that all energies are being exhausted in reducing self-esteem as opposed to improving self-esteem. There is a limit to what can be accomplished from a beaten-down self-esteem.

How do you turn this cycle around and make sure you are doing all you can to promote your self-esteem? Here is a list of things that can be done:

1. Recognize all of the good traits you have.
2. Continually add to the good traits you have.
3. Commend yourself when you have done something well.
4. Look at what you can accomplish as opposed to what you have not.
   Tomorrow is always another day.
5. Have a vision of where you are going and what you want to do.
6. Set goals on a regular basis. Write them down and celebrate your accomplishments. Start small and think long-term.
7. Look at all of the good things in your life and be thankful.

Don't take anything for granted.

8. Take the time to appreciate your loved ones, and let them know it.
9. Appreciate your job and what you can learn from it. Every job can provide a lesson or improve your skills.
10. Start your day by giving yourself a pep talk on your attributes.

The Appreciation "Apple"

Eat an Apple Daily

Apple Ingredients

- Recognize your good attributes
- Enjoy you
- Add to good traits
- Compliment self
- Keep vision within sight
- Appreciate the moment
- Appreciate your loved ones
- Appreciate what you do
- Set goals
- Be thankful
- Give yourself pep talks

Summary

Look at what you can accomplish as opposed to what you have not.

Good self-esteem allows you to make mistakes and learn.

Take responsibility for mistakes and accept them for what they are: learning opportunities.

Give proper attention to things you can impact, not things you can't change.

Chapter 11

No Regrets

Energy spent worrying about the past allows little for the present, and none for the future

Satchel Paige, one of the best pitchers in the history of baseball once said, "Don't look back; something may be gaining on you." This is a quote that has been used by many over the last fifty years and applies today as much as it did then.

The point Satchel was making was that in order to succeed, we must focus on what is in front of us. It means focusing on the present and the future. It means focusing on what you are trying to do today and what you hope to accomplish tomorrow.

Focusing on today means limiting the time you have on regretting things that you did yesterday. Don't worry about what you did yesterday. Don't spend unproductive energy fretting about what you could have done yesterday. You cannot reverse the past. **Putting regrets behind you is the tenth Way to Take Control of Your Destiny in Business and Life.**

Regrets, like anger and hatred toward others who have wronged you, do nothing to advance your present or future.

We all think of things we wish we could change. Any focus on these past bad experiences only advances our future when we can use them as a learning experience. In order to live happily and enjoy today and tomorrow, it is important to leave these events in the past, where they belong.

The impetus for most things we do should be based on moving us forward. It is the most positive approach to getting anything accomplished. Looking forward makes us focus on what we need to accomplish today to reach a certain end. It allows us to put the past in the past where it belongs.

Regrets can be emotional reflections that we use to motivate us to make necessary changes in our lives. In that context, there is some good in regrets. Regrets that keep us focused in the past can be a disservice to our today. The emotion regrets generate, to a point, is good. However, emotion that becomes a driving force behind every endeavor can allow life-altering decisions to be adversely affected. When emotion becomes the driving force, there is a tendency to overlook obvious logical variables in our decision process.

The other problem with putting too much focus on regrets is it can drain valuable energy we need today. This is what causes people to repeat the same mistakes and spend a lifetime on regrets. With energy spent on the past, the present and future never get their due focus. The cycle, as a result, perpetuates itself.

The key to leaving regrets behind is to work through the grieving process quickly, and move forward. Regret, like any other human emotion, requires one to go through the necessary steps in order to have closure. Proper closure is always a prerequisite to leaving a regrettable event where it belongs, in the past.

It is fairly easy to look at regret like a death. It is an event that triggers a number of emotional reactions that you must work through.

The five most acknowledged stages that one normally goes through to reach closure can also include regrets. They are denial, anger, negotiation with oneself in some form, depression, and finally acceptance. Every individual works through life-impacting events at his or her own pace. Regrets usually surface in the negotiation stage—"What could I have done differently?"

In simple terms, I would say the quickest way to run through the stages with regret is to first understand the basis for the regret. Unlike a death, there may not be a physical basis. It may be founded entirely on a perspective that you have trouble changing or bringing closure to.

Try to find some positive from a regrettable event at the time that it occurs. There is no event that can't have some positive redeeming value to it in some form. It may not be immediately evident. It may take some time to experience it, but you have a better chance of finding the positive if you are viewing from a positive perspective.

The second key is to attempt to learn something from the regret so that it can be left behind. It is possible for an initial regret to become a blessing in disguise just by what is learned and what transforms as a result.

The final and real way to always be able to move forward from regret is quite simple in theory, but not so easy in practice. View the regrettable events in your life as natural building blocks to better events that will happen in the future. Look at every situation as an experience that only widens your horizons and gives you wisdom. As long as you continue to use this newfound wisdom, you will limit repetition of the mistakes and improve your odds of the triumphs.

Even though Satchel Paige told us to not look back, I do believe it is good to look back, within a limited parameter. Don't allow looking back to cause you to trip and fall due to lack of focus on what is in front of you.

The Regrets Rectangle Box

Regrets are like anger and hatred—wasted energy.

They will not further your cause; they prolong pain.

Focus on today and tomorrow for enjoyment and success.

Outside the Box

Learn from regrets, be better prepared, and move on.

Use regrets as motivating sparks, light them only once.

Summary

Regrets are emotional reflections; when used in a limited context to motivate us to change, they are okay.

Everyone has things they wish they could do over. Take a better direction from what you have learned and eliminate the chances of repetition.

Energy overspent on worrying about the past leaves little fuel for the present, and none to prepare for the future.

Chapter 12

Every Rough Situation Is a Seminar

Wisdom, confidence, and strength do not come cheaply

We have the ability to learn more from rough situations and failures because they have a better chance of staying with us. The stress and self-doubt they cause makes it difficult to exorcise them out of our system. These are the events that continually sneak into our dreams years after we have supposedly moved on. Have you ever been asked to resign from your job or a project you were assigned to because a supervisor believed it just wasn't working out? Have you ever had a terrible job interview that you know caused you to lose a position that you believed you were qualified for? Have you ever had to testify in court, or been told by another person that they just were not interested in you?

These situations and events can impede your development and growth, if you let them. They can also cause recurring nightmares, if you allow it to happen. I'm sure we can all agree that experiencing rough situations and events is something we would rather stay clear of. The reality is that if we never experienced failure in any form, we would never grow as individuals or business professionals. Life is full of lessons that we can learn from and put to use. **Recognizing that every rough situation is nothing more than a free seminar is the eleventh Way to Take Control of Your Destiny in Business and Life.**

I can come up with a list of adverse experiences I have had that, at the time, I knew were going to be challenging. Knowing in advance that these experiences were not going to be enjoyable, it would have been easy to just bow out and refuse to participate.

Examples that quickly come to mind: being interrogated by attorneys on a witness stand for hours; negotiating a union contract on behalf of my company without law degree background or legal assistance; announcing to twenty-four employees without any advance notice that their jobs were eliminated immediately.

If this was not enough, I can add restructuring a regional operation for the new owner of a business. In this position as a general manager in a new city, I had to terminate twenty employees in my first week on the job. This was around 20% of the staff.

This list could go on and on, but I think you get the point. These were all experiences that I knew were going to be emotional and could cause major stress, if I allowed it to enter. Sometimes we have to do things we don't want to do. There is no choice, when it comes with the territory. Responsibility forces us sometimes to do things we are not sure we can do. We do them because we believe we are given no other option.

In many of these situations, trying to salvage some redeeming value can be difficult. The redeeming value can only come from the gained knowledge, experience, and understanding that we can put to use in the future. There are lessons that we can anticipate and there are those we can't prepare for; they just happen.

The key to making sure these situations, planned or unplanned, create some form of positive learning residual is to consciously absorb the lessons they impart. It is one thing to be subjected to a lesson, it is quite another to be able to learn from it.

There is no better seminar than working through a problem that taxes all of your skills, abilities, and patience. Better yet, these seminars that come along are ones we do not ask for, and therefore do not have to pay for. We learn much more from these seminars because they are self-induced, in some form. As such, these real-life seminars are voluntary as opposed to involuntary learning experiences.

These free seminars become the best way for us to develop

and grow. We call this experience. It increases our marketability in business, and helps our maturity process. This is how we develop confidence and garner strength to prepare us for the next challenge.

When going through a rough situation, or working through uncomfortable circumstances, it is too easy to just focus on the anxiety we are feeling. We want to wish the situation away. The problem with approaching anything with this detached perspective is that it puts up a firewall to wisdom.

Taking a knowledge-based approach to a rough situation opens you up to some positive future residuals. First and foremost, you will be better able to cope with a similar situation when it occurs. Second, you will be better equipped in the future to logically work through it. Thirdly, you have improved your odds of having better results and proper closure.

When you know you are going to be experiencing a new and trying situation, a presentation, or a confrontation, step back for a moment. In that moment, view this upcoming experience as a free seminar that can improve your skillset and marketability. You only need to pay attention, learn, and absorb. It does not get any better than that.

You might say it would be nicer to just sit on the sidelines and be an observer, as opposed to being a participant in these uncomfortable situations. It begs the question: do we learn better by experiencing something or by someone telling us how something is done? For the answer to that question, you need only go back to your childhood and early adult years. Remember when your parents or other family members tried to convey to you what they thought was in your best interests? They were speaking from experience. Getting advice from others, especially your parents because they could not possibly understand, meant nothing. You had to experience something yourself in order to learn, the hard way.

As you matured, through life's experiences, you realized at a later date that what they were trying to tell you was correct. But even though it was too late, you now had a reference point. You became armed with the wisdom to warn your kids, who also might not listen. (Funny how that cycle continually repeats itself.) There is a perfect Mark Twain quote that fits this learning situation: "When I was a boy of fourteen, my father was so ignorant I could hardly stand to have the old man around. But when I got to be twenty-one, I was astonished at how much the old man had learned in seven years."

One point to this story is that there is no replacement for learning something the hard way, through experience. That is why they call it *experience*.

It must be emphasized that it is not enough to just be subjected to these rough seminars in life; you must be paying attention. The learning becomes a building block. Like building a house from scratch, it takes one piece of wood and block of concrete at a time.

Summary

Rough situations give you opportunities for personal growth in your personal relationships and business relationships.

The best way to deal with any rough situation or event is to pay attention, learn, and recognize they are free; no monetary payment takes place.

Wisdom, confidence, and strength do not come cheaply.

Chapter 13

Exercise and Eat Healthy

Failure to meet unrealistic health goals perpetuates a "who cares?" attitude; seek moderation

It would be wonderful if we could take an hour out of our day to exercise. It would be wonderful if we could eat only healthy food every day, without exception. It would be nice if we were able to look in the mirror and see a well-toned body that was trim and fit.

Unfortunately, that is not reality. Our busy schedules, combined with the fast-food and snack food advertising we are inundated with, make it difficult to focus on exercise and healthy eating.

In reality, it is easier to ignore the pressures of eating healthy and never take the time to exercise. As such, most people react to this battle in extremes. We either focus fanatically on exercise or we make no attempt at all. **Exercising and eating healthy with realistic expectations is the twelfth Way to Take Control of Your Destiny in Business and Life.**

If you make exercise your life focus and don't allow time for other things, you compromise your ability to have a balanced life. If you eat nothing but healthy foods, you risk taking any enjoyment out of eating. Eating becomes something you have to do only because your body demands nutrition.

There is an answer to this dilemma. It incorporates the term *moderation*. It is possible to exercise in moderation. It is also possible to eat healthy most of the time and enjoy other foods that might not be as good for you.

Studies show that Americans spend nearly 15 billion dollars a year trying to get healthy through the help of diet books, weight-loss centers, and health clubs. The result is that around 65% of the population is overweight and nearly 40% is obese. How can it be that we spend so much money trying to get trim and healthy and yet be so overweight? How must we feel knowing that we are spending to an extreme to be trim and healthy and it is not working?

Does it make sense to set an extreme goal, when lowering the bar to an achievable point could make more sense? What if we were to accept looking *somewhat* trim and *fairly* healthy? Is it possible those goals are more realistic and achievable?

Anything in life done to an extreme usually has a chance of having dire consequences. If you take a look around you at examples of moderation, you will notice it has had a tendency to produce fuller enjoyment of life. A mix is never a bad thing because it produces varied experiences and gives one a fuller perspective. There is not much doubt about what a narrow perspective can do to both the interpretation of something and the enjoyment of anything. A narrow focus normally equates to a narrow experience.

Exercising and having good eating habits is a critical step to a healthier existence. As such, it should be a very important part of everyone's life. But, it does not have to be done to an extreme to be effective. Body-building exercise and a perfect body are not realistic goals for most people. Setting that kind of goal is a lot like a New Year's resolution; they go by the wayside quickly. Be realistic. Make consistency the goal. Define a consistency for exercise that is achievable and sustainable.

Exercise within moderation. Introduce it in your life as something you do three to five times a week for 20 to 30 minutes at a time. A regimented schedule is a real plus. However, having stated that, do what works for you. Have a realistic regimen that can be sustained over the long-term. It then becomes something that defines you in a small way. It is not the only way you are defined. Eat healthy within moderation. Don't shut out of your diet those non-healthy foods you enjoy eating once in a while. The exception to this, of course, would be unless your doctor recommends otherwise.

Let's look at some examples of how some activities can be done within moderation. It is possible to reduce calorie surplus by some simple actions that also align with personality.

Most people enjoy eating chocolate. It has been determined that dark chocolate is very good for you if eaten within reason. Researchers at the University of L'Aquila found that eating dark chocolate could help control diabetes and lower blood pressure. Chocolate contains antioxidants, but it also contains a lot of fat and calories.

Instead of eating a candy bar every day or every other day, how difficult would it be to reduce that need? You could reduce that chocolate intake by just eating a couple of small pieces of dark chocolate each day. By making that simple change, you would reduce your calorie intake in half while improving your chances of being healthy. An average dark chocolate candy bar has around 500 calories and 80 grams of fat. Eating two small pieces of dark chocolate instead, would reduce that intake by around 75%. The need is taken care of while the calorie intake is reduced.

The problem with most diets and health programs is that a person has to do a complete lifestyle change. By reducing according to what fits your lifestyle and personality, you can improve your health while not having to make a 180-degree change in your life. This is a win-win situation. We need win-win situations, not only because they work best over time, but also because they make us feel good.

Other examples of foods that are hard for most people to give up are fast food, ice cream, cake, and potato chips. This list is really endless. What if we made an effort to reduce our intake of high-fat foods without giving them up altogether? It seems it would be easier than trying to eliminate them entirely. It clearly is much easier to decrease the use of something than to give it up entirely.

There are many other examples of adaptable eating habit changes that don't require a complete life-altering transition. Incorporate in your lifestyle those changes that are easiest for you based on your personality. Some of those might be:

Drinking skim milk instead of 2% or 2% instead of whole milk

Eating fat-free ice cream instead of regular ice cream

Drinking coffee with one teaspoon of sugar instead of two teaspoons

Eating fast food once a week instead of two or three times a week

Trying to eat a balanced meal three times a week instead of whenever

Reducing fat foods per week by half

Drinking beer twice a week instead of three or more times a week

Cutting down on the butter you put on your potato

Eliminating snacks three hours before you go to bed

Reducing the number of nights you snack

Cutting your bread intake by half

Buying low-fat food as a mix in your diet

Reducing the number of times you eat dessert each week by half

Packing a lunch for work a few times a week

These are just a few examples of the small changes you can make that can have a significant impact on calorie intake. It is possible to reduce calories without giving up foods that you love. The idea is to do what fits your personality and lifestyle. Don't start a diet that is so life-changing and demanding that it causes resentment and results in you abandoning it entirely.

It is also possible to burn more calories on a daily basis

without making major lifestyle changes, changes that become unsustainable. Examples of ways you can burn calories without much effort include:

Mall shopping that is unorganized creates added steps

Parking in the farthest parking spot from the entrance

Walking to pick up the mail as opposed to driving up to the mailbox

Taking a lunch to work and taking a walk after eating

When working around the house, taking duplicated unnecessary steps to go from one area to the next (because we always feel rushed to get things done, we most often take the straightest path to our destination)

Mow the lawn with a mower you push as opposed to a riding mower

Rake the leaves instead of blowing them

Make a point to stand a little more at night instead of just sitting on the couch

Walk the dog instead of just letting him out

Our exercise habits continue to be impacted by convenience products and technological advances. Together they continue to reduce our physical activity. These products, which result in less physical activity or increase our fat intake, are all created in the name of saving us time.

We have not quite realized that this attempt to help us keep pace in our busy lives really does nothing to reduce our load. Have you ever noticed that it seems impossible to catch up with work and home responsibilities? One thing gets done, and more things replace it. The simple reason for this is that time does not stand still. One thing completed usually has at least two things waiting to replace it.

When we take the time to acknowledge this phenomenon, we begin to realize that putting quality time into activities and enjoying them actually has some redeeming value. Take the extra time to walk the dog instead of just letting him outside. Take those extra steps around the house when doing some activity. The gain in enjoyment and calorie expenditure will be worth the effort. Most importantly, a moderate approach to tasks as opposed to a hurried one may have some surprising benefits. There might be some enjoyment. Having said all this, it is well understood that sometimes we need to finish a task quickly. But this should not apply to everything. Moderation has its place.

You will find that through a "moderate" approach you can feel good while not feeling deprived. It will eliminate that constant rushed feeling. It may produce better results while promoting good balance in your life.

The Moderation Maker Graft
Old O
New N
*Get **ON** Board — A Little Goes a Long Way*

	N	O		N		
O			N	O	O	N
					N	O
Healthy Eats	Junk Food		Exercise		Calories In	Calories Out

Summary
Eating healthy and exercising in moderation is easier to achieve and sustain.

Moderation has a better success ratio, increases self-esteem due to success, and perpetuates consistency.

Moderation allows you to eat healthy without being deprived of foods that bring enjoyment.

Chapter 14

Don't Take Yourself Too Seriously; Take What You Do Seriously

Enjoy yourself for who you are while working on development

Around 1983 I had entered the crazy world of broadcast television as a business manager for a network affiliate. At the time, this was a television station on a very tight budget. "Cost effectiveness" was the mode of operation. In fact, this station's only vision was to maintain the status quo because the financial losses were mounting. Needless to say, our production department's goal was to create the best commercials it could at the least amount of cost. Clients were not willing to pay for producing commercials and our production department was not willing to give anything away.

There was a particular computer business that decided to use our station to begin an advertising campaign. They were in need of a fresh, cheap spot. They had just opened for business. Their budget had limitations.

The idea conceived by our very creative production manager was to feature a man from the Middle East counting camels, sheep, and goats in the desert while holding an abacus. It was believed that would get them the attention they needed as a new business.

The production manager also came up with the great idea that I would be the perfect actor for the spot. I had dark black hair and could grow a beard in minutes, unfortunately. He asked me if I would do the commercial. All I had to do was grow a beard for a few days, wear a thin robe with a turban, and shoot the spot in 30-degree temperatures on the sand dunes. It was October in northern Michigan and we were getting some occasional snow. How could anyone say no to that? I agreed to do the commercial.

My life philosophy was to always be willing to try anything once, as long as it was legal and ethical. This qualified.

To make a very long story short, the commercial ran for around three months at the cost of around $4,000 to the client. Unfortunately, after four months, we had not received a penny in payment from this client. I was aware of this because, as the business manager, I was responsible for all accounting functions. One of these responsibilities included overseeing receivables.

Five months passed without us receiving a payment from this advertiser. I contacted our attorney and asked that he start litigation against this client. After a few futile months trying to mediate a settlement, the case finally ended up in the courtroom. The computer business had an interesting reason for not paying, as conveyed to me by our attorney: "The actor in the spot was so bad, it cost them business." They were very close to closing their doors.

I did tell our attorney that the actor in the spot was me. He immediately understood why they were upset. I had never claimed to be an actor. To say the least, I had no delusional ideas of quitting my day job after the commercial hit the airwaves. The computer business closed its doors before we could ever collect a penny. This became an entertainment piece at the station for some time. Even though I was not pleased my acting efforts had turned into a write-off, I laughed when I heard someone telling the story. **Not taking yourself so seriously is the thirteenth Way to Take Control of Your Destiny in Business and Life.**

If I had taken myself too seriously and been defensive about this event, the repeated laughing this caused could have been psychologically damaging. But, I put myself in the shoes of a spectator, and as a spectator, this was a funny story, plain and simple.

Acting was hardly a career for me. I knew it clearly was not my forte. It was something I tried while accommodating a client. It was something I had never done before. It was a new experience, nothing more and nothing less.

Most people gravitate to a defensive mode when it comes to being critiqued by others for things they do. This is a common human characteristic. We all make attempts to insulate ourselves from criticism. It does not matter what the intentions of the giver are. In harmless fun or not, we still try to shield ourselves from feedback that may impact our self-esteem.

It is easy to think of oneself as an island. It is human nature to believe that only we make foolish mistakes. We are the only ones who do things that are embarrassing. Truth is, any time an individual makes an effort to interact with another, it creates an opportunity for foolishness and mistakes.

Eliminate that concern by recognizing that we all make mistakes. We all do foolish things. Allow yourself to be human; you are. Acknowledging that this is inevitable is the first step to reducing the worry of it happening. Look at any mistake or foolishness that does not kill someone as being entertaining. Be willing to laugh at yourself, and do so when it happens.

Not taking yourself so seriously eliminates the worry of making mistakes. It allows for learning from situations. It will also allow you to enjoy others more because focus is re-directed from yourself. You will see more than you have ever seen before. It is like taking the time to "smell the flowers." It can be an exhilarating experience.

There is another story that I have fond memories of. At the time, I was in my early twenties. My wife and I had only been married for one year. To understand how this ridiculous situation could unfold, I must incorporate the events leading up to it and the other character involved.

My wife and I were living in Lansing, Michigan, and owned a little dog named Bones. He was no bigger than a loaf of bread. On this particular Friday night in 1975, we had some friends over from out of town. We had been partying to the wee hours of the morning, 3:00 a.m. to be exact. Unfortunately, Bones had a doctor's appointment scheduled for around 7:30 a.m. on Saturday. The combination of getting very little sleep, in addition to being a little hungover, was the perfect recipe for a bad situation.

Bones was a cute, black-and-gray peek-a-poo who must have weighed not more than ten pounds. He always had an innocent look on his face, whether he was guilty of something or not. As such, he was always excusable because, guilty or not, it was hard to get upset at such a cute, little dog. As a result, I would say he was quite spoiled. He was fully aware of that fact. Although his being spoiled has nothing to do with this story, or the outcome, being cute and innocent-looking does.

In this particular location, where the vet had his office, there also were doctor offices for people on the other side of the parking lot. Try to picture a row of offices in the middle of a large parking lot with office fronts facing both sides. With the information I have given you so far, you may be visualizing what must have occurred.

Unfortunately, on this particular morning, I was not in the proper state to be taking a dog to the vet for his shot.

Just the same, I got into the car and drove to the vet's. Unfortunately, I parked on the wrong side of the offices. Oblivious, I walked into the wrong office. Unfortunately, my main focus, while trying to negotiate my steps, was to carry Bones without stumbling. I carried him under one arm, as you might carry a loaf of bread. I walked up to the receptionist's window.

"The name is Bones; have an appointment for seven thirty. Here to get a shot," I stated looking forward with no emotion.

"Did you say Bones?" the young lady said in a friendly reply.

"Yes, I did. Bones," I answered as my head throbbed. This was more of a conversation than I cared to have in this exhausted state.

"I'm afraid I don't see any Bones on my list for seven thirty," she quickly retorted in a sarcastic tone.

This was the first slight hint I was in the wrong place. I was not quick to pick up on it, nor did I want to.

"Stay here, while I go check with the nurse in the back," she added.

Behind me was a reception room full of patients, standing room only. I could not detect for sure, but I thought I could hear some whispering and slight chuckles. I could not say for sure. The last thing I wanted to do was confirm it by turning around. At this point, it was beginning to occur to me that I might be in the wrong office. But I was fully committed now. I was "all in" as they say in poker. I had no other choice but to stay the course, and act unaffected. I was beginning to fear what could be at the end of this interaction. I began to take on a state of what could be best described as freeze-mode. I did not move.

A few minutes later, which seemed like hours at the time, a very large and intimidating woman walked out of the back office. I assumed she was a nurse. I could tell as she opened the door to the reception area that she meant business. One way or another, this situation was going to be resolved real quickly.

"Are you the guy who says there is an appointment for a Bones scheduled for this morning?" the large nurse demanded in a commanding voice.

"Yes, I am," I answered meekly, fearing that what was going to come out of her mouth would be heard by everyone in this over-congested reception area.

"Is Bones, by chance, the dog you are holding in your arms?" she asked in a way that would have made any court attorney proud.

"Yes," I answered nervously, like a discredited witness in a courtroom whose real identity had been shockingly revealed to an astonished audience.

"Well," she stated and paused. I knew at this point that my deepest fear was about to happen. She was not going to discreetly let me out of this with any degree of dignity. She finished, "We do not take care of dogs in this office; we only take care of humans!" She unfortunately stated this in what sounded like a scream. It seemed that her intent was to make sure that everyone in the reception area could share in the moment.

I walked out of that office with my little dog in my left arm. I had a look of total humiliation, the proper look for this moment. Bones looked the part of an innocent bystander, an involuntary participant in a comedy routine. I put my head down. Bones lifted his head up, trying to interpret all the loud laughs and applause. I could not get out of that office fast enough. Needless to say, Bones did not get his shot that morning. His real appointment time on the other side of the building had passed.

I must admit that I did not tell my wife or anyone else that story for at least five years. The last thing I wanted to do was to give her the impression that the person she had married might be two cards short of a full deck.

When I finally told my wife, it was like a load had been lifted off of my shoulders. Unfortunately, she was not the last person to hear the story or tell the story. It had taken a few years, but after telling the story more than a few times, I began to really have an appreciation for it. I began to realize that crazy things can happen. They are part of what makes life entertaining. There is nothing wrong with being an entertainer. People pay big money to be entertained. It was a funny story, and as such, it was not fair to keep it from others.

Nobody is perfect. Interact with others and you will always risk doing something that makes you look silly. Fail to interact and you will miss the important times in life that make life enjoyable.

Again, allow yourself to be human. Recognize that as long as you interact with people and events, you will make mistakes.

When you start with that premise, you can laugh at yourself when the moment deserves that reaction. By not taking yourself so seriously, you are then able to enjoy yourself. It allows you to move forward from things and events that don't go as planned.

I have many other simple examples of embarrassing moments. Let me entertain you with a more recent example. Have you ever been in a meeting and accidentally misstated a word that entirely changed the meaning of your statement? Saying the secret to sex as opposed to the secret to success can create a completely different visual for both presenter and listener. I did that recently in a seminar that I was delivering to a group that included VPs and a CEO who were listening quite attentively. My quick response was, "I bet that got everyone's attention! You are now left to decide if I stated that on purpose or if it was stated intentionally to grab your attention. I'll let you decide, because I'm not telling," I added.

Was I embarrassed? Maybe, for a few seconds, but I moved forward as though it had never happened. Because I showed no embarrassment, I believe the audience was able to move forward too. During this same speech, I happened to be talking about the importance of not taking oneself so seriously. I had been explaining how important it was to accept mistakes and not torment oneself when it happens. How applicable was this mistake to the message I was delivering? I would say it became a little example of how I practice what I preach.

Taking what you do seriously is different. You should always give the proper focus, dedication, and seriousness to any endeavor. Recognize that giving your best is not a sometimes-thing; it is an all-the-time thing. Focus and look forward with the goal of doing better tomorrow because of what you have learned today. Until tomorrow, enjoy the moment. If that requires laughing at something you have done, do it.

Summary

Recognize that you will make mistakes and do foolish things at times in your life.

Enjoy yourself for who you are while working on development.

Take what you do seriously.

Chapter 15

Treat Others with Respect

Respect is the fastest way through firewalls

The best way to get respect as a person, as a manager, or as a partner in any relationship, is to treat others with respect. If you treat others as you wish to be treated, you will be amazed at the enjoyment you can get from others. It allows one to better appreciate being around others, which then goes both ways.

Respect impacts friendships. Respect impacts productivity. Respect impacts efficiency in the work environment. Respect impacts collaboration and it impacts the work environment culture significantly. It creates a better micro-work world. Respect results in success for individuals, and it results in success for companies.

Respect allows you to enjoy others for the little things they have to offer. Respect allows you to bond. It opens doors to friendships that otherwise would not exist. **Treating others with respect is the fourteenth Way to Take Control of Your Destiny in Business and Life.**

We miss out on a lot of life by not taking the time to see past the surface of people. Most people put up a firewall that prevents others from coming into their space. When we take the time to listen to people, we begin to see shared commonality not detected in a surface-to-surface interaction. When we take this time to get to know someone, the firewall breaks down.

I have always believed that it is possible to find something you have in common with everyone you meet. It is just a matter of taking the time to search out what that might be.

I use an audience-participation exercise in one of my seminars to prove this point. I have seen many people be very surprised at how much they had in common with a coworker, as well as enjoy this exercise very much.

I break up the participants into groups of two. I give each group around ten minutes to come up with at least five things they have in common that are totally non-work related. I have found that not only do they have an easy time finding five things they share; it seems to create a proactive synergy. It is as though they have found a new friend. They now know a person much better than they did before the exercise.

This is where respect is born and nurtured. We most often respect people we know and have taken the time to know better. Respect comes from getting to know an individual as opposed to just knowing them on the surface. We get to know others by getting below the surface and understanding who they really are. Respect has been earned.

In the business environment, respect is too often demanded without the earning process ever taking place. The best examples I have seen have usually involved the relationship between a new manager and his or her staff. I have seen these new managers expect respect just because their new title says they should. What they fail to realize is that respect does not come with the title. One must go through a process where it is earned.

Early in my career as a department manager in broadcasting, an individual new to the business was hired as the station manager. He had no management experience. However, his father was president of the company. Apparently that was all the experience that was necessary. He replaced the general manager who had hired me, so I was not thrilled to see this change. The previous general manager was a mentor of mine.

The new station manager, because of his name and title, expected immediate respect from the managers and staff of the station. As the business manager for the station, I worked closely with this person. I actually enjoyed working with him, but most everyone else did not feel the same. I felt the poor guy had really been put in a no-win situation. He did not have the experience necessary to succeed in this position, and his last name worked against him.

From day one of his arrival, he made it clear to all that he expected to be addressed as Mr. He also verbally made it clear he demanded respect. He had apparently never learned that respect is one thing you can't really demand. He was not willing to earn it. Within a year, the managers and staff had heard enough of his demands and sent a letter to the president making their own demands. Their demands were that his son be replaced. They had more than they could take from his guy. They had spoken with a unanimous voice. The company had no choice but to replace him. I remember this well because I was promoted to the station manager position to replace him. I still felt bad for him. He did not know any better and he was not about to learn. Other than that trait, I found him likeable.

He had learned too late that respect was something that one earns. He learned that it was not automatic, and it was not given without basis.

Respect is not something that should be taken lightly by the receiver, because it is not taken lightly by the giver in most cases.

The most meaningful respect is earned through multiple inter-actions over a period of time. Give respect the respect it deserves and you will be treated with respect.

The word *respect* is one of the most powerful words in the human dialogue and has been the basis for many battles between people of different nations, religions, races, and ethnic backgrounds. The lack of it has been the battle cry for many sports teams on the way to championships.

Respect is one of the most important, sought after achieve-ments that we can accomplish, yet it is so hard to get. If everyone recognizes its importance and wants it so badly, why are we so reluctant to give it?

I don't know the answer to that question totally. I do believe it goes back to our desire to be accepted by others. I also believe that it is one thing that gets most people's attention. It is the best way to build a relationship and get the most out of any relationship while enjoying interaction with another person.

Respecting others is a powerful tool to have in your arsenal. But it is important that it be authentic. It makes life much more interesting and enlightening when it is given to others with sincerity. It is one of the most untapped resources in the world. We all desire respect because it can have a major impact on our own self-esteem. We don't take the time to put it to its full use as much as we should.

We are so stretched from demands at work and at home, we too often just go through the motions when interacting with others. The problem with years of going through the motions is it becomes more than just a by-product of a social environment. Over a period of time, it becomes a defining characteristic of that environment.

Take the time to get to know others and respect them for who they are. This is time that will be rewarding, both in your business and personal life. There may be a reason why that person you have been trying to work with or work through has made the relationship so challenging. Add a little respect to the mix. You might be surprised at the outcome. That firewall that you have been trying to penetrate might not be as difficult to negotiate as you had believed.

The Respect Resonator

Respect... Respect Reciprocated
Respect... Enjoyment of others
Respect... Penetrates firewalls
Respect... Impacts relationships
Respect... Opens doors
Respect... Builds networks

Summary

Respect is the common denominator in finding enjoyment in others.

Real respect is earned—it does not come automatically with title or position.

Chapter 16

Life is Theatre

Sometimes we need to take a step back, and become the audience in our own show

There are times when an emotional experience is more than we can handle. During some of these emotional and physically draining times, you would like nothing more than to detach yourself from the event in order to reduce the pain. It is times like these when you should detach for another reason: to be able to see things more clearly.

When the show gets too tough to handle as a participant, take a step back and become the audience. It will put you in a better position to see a situation for what it is as opposed to what your emotions tell you it is. During these times, emotions squash your logical thinking process. This is what causes you not only to make wrong decisions, but also convert pain to suffering. Take the time to step back and detach.

Once your head is less cluttered, you will be able to see things clearer as a non-participant. You can then better work through the issue. This can be equated to what some have referred to as an "out of body experience" while near death. Consider this an awake, self-induced out of body experience. **Recognizing that life is theatre is the fifteenth Way to Take Control of Your Destiny in Business and Life.**

Another major cause of stress to most people is interaction with difficult people. In most cases, this takes place in the work environment. Be entertained as opposed to being offended or upset when dealing with difficult people. Some people are just more difficult to get along with. Other people are simply more easy-going. Sometimes it has to do with a person's personality.

Other times it just might be a by-product of other issues.

Life is extremely entertaining when you take the time to see things as a non-participant. Instead of being irritated by something or someone, be entertained by it. See the humor in the predictability. Life has many moments that we just don't take the time to laugh about because we are too emotionally attached or affected by the situation.

Step back and make believe you are on a stage. Just remove yourself from the show. You are now the audience. Be ready to laugh and applaud, and be armed with immunity when you jump back into the show. Some people would define this kind of reaction as having schizophrenic tendencies. I define it as an avenue to stability.

Taking a step back does not eliminate any exposure you may have to difficult situations. It doesn't even completely eliminate the stress or emotional abuse you may feel. It is, however, a means of reducing the impact and stress. It also allows you to control the emotional high that you may be under. This, in itself, can reduce the chances you will say something you might regret. It also can reduce your chances of making dramatic decisions based entirely on emotion.

One of the major rules I live by in life is to not make life-altering decisions during major emotional moments or during major transitional times. That does not mean you should not make *any* decisions during these emotional peaks. Great change and events have happened in history as a result of this mix. This does not mean that you should not take risks, because you should. You should just make sure your decisions and the risks you take have some logical foundation as well as the necessary emotion to move forward.

I have seen people make major life-changing decisions based entirely on emotion. Most often this results in complicating a situation. What was a bad situation becomes a catastrophic situation; one that becomes even more difficult to recover from.

A prime example of this is a person who quits a successful job he has enjoyed because of a short-term adversity at work. Months later, when he realizes it was just a minor bump, he is on the outside looking in. That door is now closed.

Sometimes you just have to detach yourself from a situation in order to release the emotion and get a more logical perspective. When the show gets too tough to handle and you need a "grounded" analysis, step out. This will allow you to achieve a more objective and logical view for deciding the direction you need to take. The show will certainly not go anywhere when you take a different view from the balcony or front row.

After you have finished your popcorn and beverage, jump back in. You'll enjoy the zest and calmness you provide in the next act.

Summary

Take time to step back. Sometimes this gives you a clearer picture.

Detaching yourself allows you to see a situation from a more logical perspective and reduce the emotion.

Detaching allows you to be entertained.

Become the audience in your own show.

**BUSINESS
BOOKS**

Business Books encapsulates the freshest thinkers and the most successful practitioners in the areas of marketing, management, economics, finance and accounting, sustainable and ethical business, heart business, people management, leadership, motivation, biographies, business recovery and development and personal/executive development.